Remember Guam

A collection of
memories and recipes
to warm your heart and lighten your spirit

Paula Ann Lujan Quinene

INFINITY
PUBLISHING.COM

Copyright © 2009 by Paula Ann Lujan Quinene

ISBN 0-7414-5503-X

Published by:

1094 New DeHaven Street, Suite 100

West Conshohocken, PA 19428-2713

Info@buybooksontheweb.com
www.buybooksontheweb.com
Toll-free (877) BUY BOOK
Local Phone (610) 941-9999
Fax (610) 941-9959

Printed in the United States of America
Published July 2009

In memory of my uncles,

Raymond Manibusan LeFever
Jesse San Augustin Cruz
Gregorio Lujan Cabe

my aunt,

Margarite Lujan

and my cousins,

Thomas Edward Cabe Diaz
Randy Raymond Cabe LeFever

Dedication

This book is dedicated to my children, Carson Edward Lujan Quinene and Evalie Ann Lujan Quinene. May you both remember Guam through your own experiences with every visit to grandma and grandpa's house. Life on Guam will not be for you as it was for me. However, I hope I do my job well as a parent to instill in you the values that have been passed down from one Chamorro generation to the next. Values that are upheld on Guam and abroad as a proud Chamorro should carry on: respect for your elders, your parents, and an unrelenting spirit of giving and sharing.

Felix P. Camacho
Governor

Michael W. Cruz, M.D.
Lieutenant Governor

A MESSAGE FROM THE GOVERNOR AND LIEUTENANT GOVERNOR OF GUAM

Hafa Adai! Congratulations on the successful publication of the book "Remember Guam."

As an island that continues to highlight and perpetuate the tradition of story-telling about local history, it is imperative that we recognize the importance of preserving these stories. The cultural values, politics, legends, beliefs and lifestyle expressed through the story-telling experience exemplify the very core of what is unique to the Chamorro people.

It is through your unwavering dedication and commitment of time to publishing this compilation of stories that provides us with another way in which we can celebrate Guam and her people. We commend you for all you have done for our community.

The history of our island and its culture will be enjoyed by people today and future generations. We are proud of the publication "Remember Guam" and look forward to the continued inspiration you bring to the people of our region and the world.

Congratulations and *un dangkolo na Si Yu'us Ma'ase!*

Sinseru yan Magåhet,

FELIX P. CAMACHO
I Maga' Låhen Guåhan
Governor of Guam

MICHAEL W. CRUZ, M.D.
I Segundo Na Maga' Låhen Guåhan
Lieutenant Governor of Guam

Table of Contents

Acknowledgments

My thanks to the man, my husband, Edward J. Quinene, for all his help with the pictures and editing the videos! He also took the front cover and inside photos during our trips to Guam in 2000 and 2006.

My thanks to my mom, Maureen Ann Cruz Lujan, my sister, Pearl Lujan Ungacta, and my friend, Fe Cruz Thornton, for editing my book!

Thank you also to my mother-in-law, Dolores Jeanette Quintanilla Quinene (a.k.a. Mom Q), my mom and my dad, Maureen & Paul Lujan, for helping me with and sharing their recipes!

Thank you to John P. Rabon, T.C. Dailey, and Clyde Hoggan for sharing their pictures! I will treasure them always!

Thank you, to all of you who took the time to share your memories, your stories, and your photos!

Hafa Adai!

A major portion of this book is dedicated to the collection of memories and stories I have received from people all over the world. These stories have been divided into decades: 40's, 50's, 60's, etc., as well as places, events, and traditions. There are stories from veterans who served during WWII, from folks who were stationed on Guam recently, from those who found work there for a few years, from those young ladies who were whisked away, married and have been unable to return home, from those still living on Guam, etc.

It's ok to be sad, to miss what life used to be, to yearn for the wonderful time you and I had on Guam: at least we have our memories, in print, to share and preserve for all time!

Another portion of "Remember Guam" is dedicated to our food! I LOVE GUAM FOOD! I have taken it upon myself to strive to record the foods we love such that future generations can enjoy them! I am terribly disturbed when individuals do not share, or even worse, intentionally give an incorrect recipe! The writing of this book is just the beginning of what is proving to be a very fun and rewarding endeavor! Visit www.paulaq.com for a video of each recipe. See page 123 for video instructions.

On the next few pages you will find pronunciation guides. This should help you with some of the words found throughout the book.

At the end of the book you will find a short excerpt of my next project, *Chamorrita Passions*. Yes, it is a historical romance novel. Once upon a time, I was able to read a great many books, though they were romance novels instead of Harry Potter. I figured this would be a wonderful opportunity to put Guam's history into a context that would be a little more exciting to read. A book more inviting than a plain, old history book.

The Chamorro Alphabet

The Chamorro alphabet is not simply A, B, C, D, etc. When we say the alphabet, we say it in terms of the sound of the letters: glotta, a, aw, be, che, de, ge, he, fe...where the 'e' takes on the short sound. Note that there is no 'J, Q, V, W, X, or Z' in the Chamorro language. The special characters in the Chamorro alphabet are the glotta ('), the lonat (°), and the enye (~). The glotta is used to stress a syllable in the word. Words using the lonat (°) above the letter 'a' make the sound "aw." Words using the enye (~) over the letter 'n' make the sound "nye."

Chamorro letter – Chamorro word – English translation

Glotta (glo-ta)

Aa
Aga (a-ga) – banana

Å
Åbas (aw-bas) – guava

Bb
Boñelos (bo-nye-lus) – doughnut

Ch
Chandia (tsan-dee-ya) – watermelon

Dd
Dågo (daw-goo) – yam

Ee
Eskabechi (es-ka-be-tsee) – fried fish with veggies

Ff
Fanihi (fa-knee-he) – fruit bat

Gg
Gåmson (gawm-son) – octopus

Hh
Halu'u (ha-lew-ew) – shark

Ii
Iba (ee-ba) – local sour "cherry"

Kk
Kåddo (kaw-do) – soup

Ll
Lemmai (lem-my) – breadfruit

Mm
Mansåna (man-saw-na) – apple

Nn
Niyok (knee-dzuk) – coconut

Ñ
Ñålang (nyaw-lang) – hungry

Ng
Nang'ga (nang-ga) – wait

Oo

Ora (o-ra) – time

Pp

Papåya (pa-paw-dza) – papaya

Rr

Rosa (ro-sa) – rose

Ss

Siya (see-dza) – chair

Tt

Tano (ta-nugh) – land

Uu

Ubas (uw-bas) – grapes

Yy

Yengyung (dzeng-dzung) - shake

English pronunciation guide to a few "hard to pronounce" villages / places on Guam

This is not a list of the villages of Guam, though most are noted. This is simply a layman's guide to commonly mispronounced names.

Adelupe (a-de-loop)

Agana (a-ga-nya)

Agana Heights (a-ga-nya   heights)

Anigua (a-nee-gwa)

Barrigada (ba-ree-gaw-da)

Canada (ka-nyaw-da)

Chalan Pago (cha-lan   paw-go)

Dededo (de-dee-doe)

Inarajan (i-na-raw-hawn)

Ipan (ee-pan)

Leyang (le-dzang)

Maina (ma-ee-na)

Maite (my-tee)

Malojloj (ma-low-luw)

Merizo (mur-eets-oh)

Mongmong (mong-mung)

Ordot (or-dut)

Piti (pee-tee)

Sinajana (Si-na-han-ya)

Sumay (sue-my)

Talofofo (ta-low-fogh-fugh)

Tiyan (tee-dzan)

Toto (togh-tugh)

Tumon (too-mon)

Umatac (you-ma-tack)

Yigo (jee-go)

Yona (dzo-nya)

Foreword

Memories from the author....

Here I am: a brown eyed girl, all of 33 years young. My life in the mainland has been rewarding. It is true what they say, why people come to America: it is the land of opportunity. I am grateful and blessed for all I have accomplished since I left my tiny island in the Pacific, my island of Guam.

I was off to college at the University of Oregon in December 1992. During the middle of my college career, I reached a turning point. I was so mahålang (homesick) and classes were getting tougher. I could not afford another ticket home for the summer. I had to decide whether I should go back home to the family / friends that I missed dearly and finish at the University of Guam or stay on at the U of O and graduate with my Exercise Science degree. I had three years left in Oregon. I made up my mind to finish what I had started. I put away the Chamorro music, made Chamorro food less often, and kept myself very busy. Finally, I had only one year left of school then I could go home!

I was in my last year of college when I "met" my husband, Edward J. Quinene (a.k.a. Sonny). We were married on December 20, 1996. I followed him to his duty station in Germany. It hit me hard when I realized what I had done! I fell in love with a great guy….but, I was not going home! Our first year in Germany was a difficult year at best. Many things were quite new to me: marriage, a different country, a college graduate, a military spouse. My biggest realization was that I was not going to Guam! I cried almost every night. I had planned and worked so hard to get through the last three years of college! The joys of love and marriage worked its magic. I kept myself busy with multiple jobs and volunteer work in Germany. Finally, my husband and I were able to go to Guam in December 1999. It had been 5.5 years since I was last home.

We returned to the mainland to settle in Cary, NC in November 2000. Again, I was quite industrious……keeping busy and denial were my best defenses against being homesick.

Our next visit to Guam was in February 2006, a lapse of over 6 years. Just before we left, my sister and I were at Barnes & Noble. I was pretty sure there were no Guam cookbooks on the shelves, but looked through the books anyways. I told Pearl that I was going to be the first to write a Guam cookbook that was published nationally. Once we returned from Guam, I started work on the cookbook. *A Taste of Guam* was my way of preserving my heritage and sharing it with others. I also realized along the way that it was a better tool for me in coping with the fact that I am not living on my island. *A Taste of Guam* was published in July 2006.

I remember sitting on my bed and announcing to my husband that I was going to work on another Guam book. *Remember Guam* came to mind. I envisioned a collection of memories from people all over the world. I decided I would ask folks "What do you remember about Guam?" and publish it in one book. I felt I would be the richest person in the world to have all those memories. I believed it would be a great way to preserve memories for time immemorial, for generations to share, for us to reminisce about life on Guam.

Here are my memories. Won't you come back home with me?!

I remember......

...riding in my dad's yellow truck. He would drive into the "bushes" on Tumon Bay and come upon a clearing on the beach. Bumbpity bump we went, parking practically anywhere. Gone are those days, now replaced by hotel upon hotel.

...being at the sport-o-dome cockfight parking lot at 2 a.m. waiting for Grandpa Cabe to get off of work. He was a police officer patrolling the dome.

...slipping and sliding on baby powder in the spare room at Grandma Cabe's.....somebody got in trouble....but it wasn't me!

...the dirt road going to Grandma Cabe's house. It used to be so scary driving through there at night, especially after all the stories the grown ups would tell us: taotaomonas (people of the before time.....they really do exist!), the white lady etc.

...going to the boat basin with my family. My dad would fish. Mom and the kids would hang out.

...during the Christmas season, spending every Christmas Eve at Grandma Cruz's nobena: the beginning of her nine nights of song and prayer.

...the humongous fiestas Grandma and Grandpa Cruz's side of the family would have. There were so many people and the food was ALWAYS out of this world!

...Grandma Cruz getting real busy during the holidays. She was a techa in her younger years (someone who sings / prays the rosary).....friends / family would ask her to sing and pray at their nobenas.

...the Yigo Amusement Park being open for the summer carnival....though it would be closed more than open for most of its life. I am not sure if it is even still standing today, lonesome behind what used to be Ben Franklin Department Store.

…Ben Franklin in Tamuning, the one stop shop for everything. The first floor had groceries and household stuff, the second through 4th floors had clothing, and the 5th floor had home goods.

…Town House, well, what was Town House through the 90's. Our stores on Guam were major landmarks for us because for so long, they were the only places to shop and hang out.

…when F.B.L.G. was an elementary school. We had huge fields to play Chinese jump rope and celebrate Chamorro week.

…making "diabetic" cookies with my childhood best friend, Jennifer Ann Taitano Cruz. We experimented much with ingredients coming up with "Tootsie Roll" cookies and something with M&M's.

…when it was safe to play in the streets. Jen and her siblings, my siblings and I, and our other neighborhood friends (Salas, Quintanilla, Infiesto, Quenga, Cura, Toves) used to play kickball, dodge ball……or just sit on the sidewalk waiting for our parents to yell at us.

…Gibson's. I didn't have much money to shop in the tourist area, but, I loved the tiny bakery stand in there, and the arcade at the end of the strip. This was my pit stop on my walk from Clark Hatch (then Pacific Star Hotel, now Marriott) to the staircase off the cliff…..on East Agana Bay.

…how much pain my calves were in after doing that staircase 10 times!! It was a great challenge!

…Cool Spot, where you could get the best tacos on Guam!!

…Julian Infiesto. I had a childhood crush on him. He was my next door neighbor. Julian was one of the nicest boys I have ever met. I think of him now and then. He passed away a few years ago. I guess it was time for him to go home. He was my brother Jun's best friend.

…my freshman year at Simon Sanchez High School: there was this girl wearing stockings for P.E. It was hilarious! She is now one of my nearest and dearest best friends, Melonie Benavente Quintanilla.

…babysitting two of the cutest little boys, Gene-Phillip & Sean-Joaquin Cruz Thornton. I remember sitting in the passenger side of the car, my window down, Sean behind me in his car-seat. I told his mom, Fe, "look, he is really laughing!" Poor kid, he was just trying to catch his breath!

…many treks up Mount Jumuyong Månglo…the one with the crosses on the top. I did it because it's just one of those things you do on Guam. I remember one climb I brought Melonie Q. with me and she advised I add vinegar to the tuna for tuna sandwiches….it would keep it from spoiling. Since then, I have always added vinegar…gives it a nice zing.

…Clark Hatch Fitness Center and Gary Miguel. It was a great place to work and workout. Gary is the best boss I have had. I made another best friend there, Cheryl Silvas, now Meregillano. Cheryl would come for hours to the gym: half the time we would talk, the other half she would run / workout.

…going for a nice beach walk before opening up the gym on Saturday mornings.

…my very first and beautiful starlit drive at 6 a.m. (February 2006) from my house in Yigo to Chotde in Anigua. This was my first time to drive on Guam (mind you I learned to drive in Mannheim, Germany when I was 23 years old). I could not wait for this morning: I was going to get some goodies and deliver it to grandma's house. It was the most tranquil morning ever, me and the road, home at last!

Remember Guam

This book belongs to

Emily C. Cruyn

Today's date is

Aug 7, 2012

Here is what I remember about Guam:

I Remember

You
Remember

We Remember

The 1940's

In the 1940's…..

- **Nov. 3, 1940** – the strongest typhoon to hit Guam since 1918. It had wind gusts exceeding 13 knots. *(Sanchez, pg. 146)*
- **April 1941** – Navy Captain George McMillin became Governor of Guam. *(Sanchez, pg. 146)*
- **Before the Japanese invasion – by December 1941,** there were 155 Chamorro teachers in 32 public schools. *(Sanchez, pg. 154)*
- **December 8, 1941** – Japan invades Guam. *(Guam History class)*
- **July 21, 1944** – America recaptures Guam. *(Guam History lass)*
- **Post WWII** – The brown tree snake finds its way to Guam. It is a native species of Australia, Papua New Guinea, and Melanesia. This predator is thought to have stowed-away on a cargo ship from the South Pacific. *(Wikipedia)*

This review is of a young girl's research on her two grandfathers: one fighting WWII in the Pacific, the other in Europe.

The following is my summary of a portion of **Jayna Kellner's** article, ***Opposite Sides of the World.*** Jayna is the niece of one of my personal training clients, John Kellner (who gave me the article). It was John's dad, also John Kellner, who fought on Guam during WWII. John Kellner senior was a young boy from Pittsburgh, Pennsylvania, part of a group known as the Statue of Liberty boys.

John was assigned to the 77th Infantry Division of the US Army, 242nd Battalion, C Company, slated to invade Guam and liberate the island from the Japanese, July 21 – August 10, 1944.

Jayna states that in one of the few stories told by her grandfather, "The landings were one of the worst parts of the battle. After the men were unloaded, those landing boats left, and there was nowhere to go but forward. The sea was behind you and the Japanese were in front of you."

Jayna writes that Corporal Kellner, serving under one of the engineer combat battalions, probably assisted in getting supplies onto the island. Jayna indicates from her research that this was quite a feat: mud, rain, limited storage sites due to difficult terrain.

In her article, Jayna compares the experience of Captain William T. Paull, USMC, Ret. to what her grandfather may have also lived through on Guam once the island was declared secure: working guard duty to prevent hiding Japanese soldiers from throwing grenades on sleeping troops, getting spooked out from rats rustling the leaves, hoping not to get a bayonet pushed into his back.

Jayna Kellner

I remember...

What do I remember about Guam? The unfortunate things I recall about my being on Guam during the invasion were the dreaded mosquitoes that carried malaria to many of our forces. Secondly, I remember the muddy roads we had to travel on....they were created by the heavy rain Guam had been having.

I recall how sad I felt for the people of Guam living in conditions of ruin. The people were very helpful and easy to make friends with. In most cases, there were areas that were out-of-bounds to us. It isolated us from going into the villages to really make friends of the masses. We did make close ties with the men and boys that came into our area so that they could help in many ways.

It pleases me to know that I took part in the liberation of Guam in 1944. Today, I feel like I have helped to restore Guam to the rightful leaders. My life has not been a waste because of the liberation and my association with the people of Guam. I am pleased that Guam has rebuilt the areas that had been destroyed. I only wish that I could afford to return for a visit.

Thank you for letting me put out a few words about the island I helped liberate and lived for over a year.

Warren Tibbitts (now 81 years old and in good health)
Whitehall, Michigan

An interview with William Robert Allen
2nd Battalion, 3rd Marine Division, 1944

I interviewed William at his home in Fuquay Varina, North Carolina. He had read an article about me and my cookbook. He contacted the local paper. It was a true blessing to meet William. He had very fond memories about his time on Guam. He had a beautiful album of some old Guam pictures. William carried this album in his sea bag and brought it to Guam, adding his Guam pictures to it.

William is originally from the Jersey / New York area. He showed me a memory book created from children of East Brook Middle School in Paramus, New Jersey. The children created memory books for veterans thanking them for their service. William was visibly touched and grateful for their thoughtfulness.

I arrived on Guam right after the initial invasion. My grandma sent me morning glory seeds. I remember one man. His name was Ignacio Iglesias Tenorio. He was 25 years old. Ignacio lived on a hill near the capital on Guam. His kids had big ulcers on their legs, jungle rot.

I was sent to Iwo Jima. I was a corpsman on the ship and never left the ship. I treated the wounded out of Iwo Jima. We buried men in the ocean. I was sent home after they dropped the Atomic bomb on Hiroshima.

Below is an article written by William's oldest daughter, Michele Dexter. The article was given to me and is reprinted as is with permission from William.

"It was 1944 in a camp opposite the Baragoda Village in Guam. My dad, William Allen, was 18. He was serving as a Pharmacist 3rd Class with the 3rd Marine Division. They were replacement troops. Their job was to patrol the island. While he was there, his 85-year-old grandmother, Frances Wetherbee, sent him morning glory seeds from her garden. Before enlisting, my dad had spent every summer on Long Island helping his grandmother plant and care for all of her gardens and her chickens. He planted the flower seeds next to the tent that he shared with eight other guys. The vines grew up and over the tent. He said the flowers were very pretty. About that time, he was sent to Iwo Jima. He said that when they left the tents were still standing. They had to hike 25 miles, with full packs, to the harbor to meet the ship. As the Corpsman, he had to walk back and forth during the hike to help those who couldn't make it. He figures that he walked more than the 25 miles. His feet were full of this "jungle rot" (as he called it) and he said his feet felt gushy the whole way. He mentioned that he treated a lot of this jungle rot with mercurochrome. He said the men got this fungus everywhere their bodies would sweat. When they boarded the ship, his feet were bleeding. He remembers two days of bare feet on the ship and the salt air cleared them up nicely. When they were on Iwo Jima, the troops were told not to call for my dad "doc" or "medic" because the enemy would shoot at him."

William Robert Allen
Fuquay-Varina, North Carolina

I remember…

I remember hearing my dad talk about having to protect the hospital and his scout sniper buddy. They flipped a coin to see who would go back for ammunition. His buddy had to go. He came back with the ammunition. My dad was talking to him, but he didn't respond. He was dead. The sniper buddy made it back to dad to give him the ammunition with a knife in him.

Dave Kalen
Saline, MI

I remember…

My father, Peter J. Murphy, was born on November 23, 1924, in Louisville, Kentucky. He graduated from St. Xavier (Catholic) High School in 1942. He enlisted in the Marine Corps on 22 February 1943, where he trained to be a radio operator in tanks.

According to his discharge papers, my father was in the Battle of Guam from 21 July 1944 to 15 August 1944.

My father passed away in 1987 and said very little about what he did in the war. My dad did say that he and his outfit made a combat landing on Guam during WWII in a Sherman tank. He was a Marine with Company B, 3rd Tank Battalion, 3rd Marine Division.

Good luck with your book. I'd like to read it some day! Thank you!

Peter J. Murphy
(Submitted by his son, Dan Murphy)

I remember…

I was born on March 3, 1932. Guam is beautiful! I lived in Inarajan village and stayed there with my kids. I remember going to school I played softball and a little bit of basketball. They liked me because I was so skinny and so fast.

I have eight sisters and we never fight. I am the oldest. I love my sisters. We all get together with our children and grandchildren. I have three brothers, but they passed away. My sisters and I, we sit down and watch our children do the work. I like to clean the house and iron – that's my favorite.

I don't like to eat – just smoke, drink my coffee and Pepsi, and eat candy. I didn't like to cook. Only my mother cooked.

The climate on Guam is very nice, not very hot, not very cold. I have ten kids, five boys and five girls. My oldest is fifty-eight.

Anita Naputi
Inarajan, Guam

I remember…

I remember our custom of helping people. When it is your turn to help, don't be afraid. I will never forget those who helped me out even for a sandwich.

I remember making kalamai, guyuria, empanada, and åhu. I remember making coconut candy – you know they melt the sugar first, then grate the niyok *(coconut)*. When the sugar melted, they mix it together. That was our candy in those days.

Mary Perez
Originally from Mangilao, Guam
Currently residing in Orlando, FL

The 1950's

In the 1950's…..

- **July 26, 1950** – The United States Congress passes the Organic Act of Guam. This gives Guamanians U.S. citizenship and a civilian government. *(Sanchez, pg. 302)*
- **January 1951** – The First Guam Legislature opened its first regular session. *(Sanchez, pg. 322)*
- **July 19, 1952** – Gladys Mae Lujan Lizama is crowned the first Guam Liberation Day Queen. *(Pacific Daily News, pg. 30)*
- **June 1952** – The Territorial College of Guam was established as a two year teacher-training school, later to be renamed as the University of Guam in 1968. *(UOG)*

Memories from my father-in-law

Edward Mata Quinene

At one time, our farm supported the Navy and Air Force commissaries with fruits and vegetables. We grew Kentucky beans, long beans, corns, watermelons, cantaloupes, honey dews, green onions, and egg plants. We had the farm at least until I joined the Marines.

We had a farm / plantation in two places. One was in Sumay. The other farm was close to our house in Merizo. We built a five bedroom, concrete house with the money from the farm.

We watered our plantation using the river water via a water pump. We would stretch the fire hose and fill up the 55 gallon drum with water.

I went to Catholic school from the 1st through the 12th grade. I was at Mt. Carmel for elementary and middle school. I attended Father Dueñas High School.

Most of the time, we had rice and kåddo for breakfast, lunch, and dinner. We bought rice from the store and raised our own chickens, pigs, and cows.

We did have fiestas at that time. We used to always have boñelos dågo at parties.

Edward M. Quinene
Originally from Merizo, Guam
Currently residing in Holly Springs, NC

I remember…

The sheer beauty of Guam and being able to be there made for one of the best times of my life. To be able to live with those memories is a privilege. I have included all of the slides from Guam, plus the CD. You may be able to use some of the Anderson AFB slides. I'm sure it has changed considerably. The slides are yours to use as you want. They are my gift to one of the most enjoyable and informative times of my life. Thank you!

Clyde Hoggan

Paula's Note: Clyde replied to my initial email request for stories in 2006. In his reply, he mentioned he had some slides that he'd love to share with me. I followed up with Clyde mid 2008. I wish you all could have heard me when I opened up a box of See's Candy....or what appeared to be See's Candy. I thought to myself, "Who in the world would send me my most FAVORITE candy, and two pounds of it?" I opened the box to find slides and a CD. You would have thought I won the lottery.....especially while I was watching the CD slide show! THANK YOU CLYDE!!

I remember…

I was nineteen years old when I met my future husband. He was in the Navy stationed at Guam Naval Hospital. We got married a few months later in September 1956. We left the island in November of that year aboard the navy ship USS ALTMAN. We stayed in St. Paul, Minnesota where he was originally from. I was married to one beautiful Italian man. He passed away seven years ago from cancer attributed to agent orange while stationed in Vietnam.

What I can remember of our beautiful island growing up was I lived in Aspengao, Barrigada with my family. I am the second youngest of nine children and my beautiful mother, Maria Leon Guerrero Cruz raised us up without our dad. My dad was killed by a couple of Japanese soldiers during the second day of invasion on the island. I had a loving and comfortable childhood. I attended elementary and high school on Guam. We have the most beautiful sunsets and clean beaches on Guam. I can remember the soft breezes and the lovely smell of the flowers at night.

I love our tropical island. I think we have the nicest and most beautiful island in the Pacific. It is enriched with the most beautiful, hospitable people who have a deep sense of culture. Such a beautiful blend….

Ms. Lola Cruz Ferrozo, 70 years old
AKA Dolores Lola Leon Guerrero Cruz
Currently residing in Aurora, Colorado

I remember…

One of the fondest memories I have are our annual trips to the homes of relatives to celebrate their village patron saint's feast day. We would travel from Asan to see the Whites in Mangilao (Santa Teresita), the Leon Guerreros in Tamuning (San Antonio), Yona (San Francisco), and Barrigada (San Vicente), and lastly to see the Taijitos in Agat (Santa Rosa). We would attend the "lukao" on Saturday. Then, we would help out with the cooking. I got to meet and know who my great aunts, uncles, and 2nd / 3rd cousins were. I still keep in touch with a lot of them to this day.

Another memory is the Camp Asan outdoor theater. Entry to the theater requires a military or Civil Service ID card. My wife, Eleanor Rojas, was a navy dependant so she vouched for me many times. Most of the Asan teens would watch movies by asking someone with an ID card. I saw movies I would not have been able to afford to see at the Johnston Theater in Tamuning.

Juan Taijito Jesus
Originally from Asan
Currently residing in Bellevue, Nebraska

I remember…

I grew up in the village of Agat. My fondest memories was of being raised on the farm. My father was from Sinajana and my mom grew up in Agana, the Belibic area. I loved those days when we used to swim in the river right behind our house. We had orchards of mango trees, avocados, and orange trees. My mom and dad also planted lots of beautiful, double "arosat" flowers called hibiscus. I just cannot get over its beautiful colors.

My father would set traps for the shrimp in the river. We would have them for days and days. Everything we ate was grown or raised right in our backyard. You might say we ate all organic foods.

I love how we party and meet all the "man-åmkos!" You better kiss their hands or fan-nginge' or else. This is how we pay respect to our elders.

I love the smell of rice and titiyas cooked in the open fire. It's like having a bond fire night after night. The sound of the children playing hide 'n seek right before dusk, was wonderful.

I remember the discipline instilled in us during the Lenten season when you are not allowed to play, make noise, or even disobey. Yes, you might get away with it then, but wait when Easter Sunday comes. We would all go to church and as soon as we got home, we got spanked for all the mischief collected during the Lenten season. This is called "paskua." We expected this and then afterwards, we all gathered for a big Easter feast.

I love and miss all these traditions encrypted in my childhood days. I have learned many values and have great memories growing up on Guam. I attended private schools all through my twelve years of schooling. I will never forget such things for as long as I live.

My mom is still alive at 89 years and lives in Las Vegas. Thank you, Paula, for allowing me to share a piece of my "Guam Memories."

Dee Crisostomo
Originally from Agat, Currently residing in Maryland

The 1960's

In the 1960's…..

- **1962** – The Naval Clearing Act is lifted by J.F.K. This opened Guam's ports to foreign and domestic visitors. *(Sanchez, pg. 339)*
- **November 11, 1962** – Super Typhoon Karen stormed over Guam. It was reported to have had two eye-walls. Super Typhoon Karen made a direct hit over Guam. She had winds of 160 mph, with gusts up to 207 mph. *(Wikipedia)*
- **1968** – The Elective Governor Act allowed Guam residents to vote for their own governor. *(Sanchez, pg. 355)*

Memories from my mom
Maureen Ann Cruz Lujan

I attended the elementary school in Sinajana (now CL Taitano Elem.) for grades K-4th (1958-1963) and 6th (1964-1965). My first grade teacher was Mrs. Castro, third grade was Mrs. Bamba, fourth grade Mrs. Villagomez....they were some of the best teachers that taught there. They made learning fun. The classrooms were clean and cool; we had fans then. I remember bringing lots of books home to do homework.

There was a store near the school, Tan Rosario's store. It was our breakfast and our lunch hangout. We'd buy bread pudding, cream puff, salty seed, sweet and sour seed, candy, coke, daigo, soup, pixie sticks, gum, etc. Somehow we had enough money then.

Some of us would go to Eskuelan Påle *(Sunday prayer school)*. We'd walk to St. Jude Thaddeus School, now Bishop Baumgartner. There was Cool Spot near Bishop. It was a great place to get cool pops.

I went to P.C. Lujan for my 5th grade year. I mostly remember the maypole in the playground. That was so much fun, but dangerous. It was a very tall pole with about 10 or so chains hanging down that you could hold on to. We'd run and lift our feet so that we'd be hanging and going around the pole. Of course, we'd have to run in unison with the other kids on the chain. I think they took that down years later. Mr. Mendiola was my teacher. I must have been a challenge for him because I felt the ruler more than once!

I attended St. Jude my 7th grade year. The nuns were not bad. I can still remember the faces of Sister Marta, Sister Clement Ann, Sister Optata, and Sister Jeremy. Sister Jeremy was the one you wouldn't want upset with you.

My junior and senior years were spent at GWSH. Those years were so so. I did enjoy high school though. I do remember the student demonstration led by Frank "Country" Reyes and Terry Fejeran. I played softball for the school, participated in a couple of clubs, and was a member of the National Honor Society. I graduated in the top 22 of my class of 500 +/- students.

I remember back in the sixties those little mom and pop stores were a delight, at least for me. You could buy Coca-Cola and daigo for a few cents. They were also close to home, a walking distance. I remember Tan Oba, Gallo, Castro, Tan Rosario's, stores in Sinajana to name a few. I know I've missed some…trying to jog my memory for names.

Those were the days. Walking the streets to visit family / friends down the road or a few blocks away was safe. Now, you have to watch your back and front.

I also remember playing under the houses called "på'pa såtgi." We used to find all kinds of treasures hidden under the houses…money mostly, unwanted items that can be used to "play house."

School was a blast for me. Before they put the fences up, we would play in the playground and the steps behind the school. I remember my grandmother dancing the båtsu at the cafeteria on those nights when they had events scheduled.

These were the years of parachute home shelters, shots, family get togethers, and laundry in the river. The parachutes became the tents for parties – they were prized possessions.

At Christmas time, the navy would come around with toys and bring a truck with Santa Claus. I remember getting toys. They came with truck loads of clothing, gifts, food. They were not cheap clothes, they were good clothes. Each village had these truck loads.

In 1970, we lived in Sinajana with my aunt, Modesta Roberto, and her family for part of the year. We had just returned from the mainland. Families lived close by. They were just a stones throw away or on the next block.

I remember referring to an area as Block 1, Lt. 2. We didn't have house numbers at the time. After the 70's, we had the urban renewal. Now you have street names and house numbers. Schools were still pretty safe. Fences were erected sometime in the 80's or so.

I remember a field trip to the Limestone Forest which is on the cliff side of George Washington Senior High. The view from the cliff was just breathtaking.

Early in 1971, the family moved to Canada (ka-nyaw-da), Barrigada. It was mostly jungle back then. We stayed at my dad's sister's house. Maman Biha was to our right, Uncle Pepe at the front, Auntie Nang at the back, Nan Ocha further down.

There were two stores in Canada: Taitano's (Tun Frank) and one near the Toto-Canada road. There's also the San Ramon Chapel (the patron saint for pregnant women). The chapel has gone through so many structural changes. It was constructed of corrugated tin and wooden poles with walls protecting the altar. Now, it's a cement structure and well tended by parishioners.

Senior trips to Gabgab Beach at Big Navy and Jones Beach in Ipan were so much fun. I'm not sure if the two are in existence today. These two areas were accessible by request or permission. They were well kept and maintained.

I met Paula's dad just before high school graduation and dated him / got married a year later on Veteran's Day.

GWSH had 523 graduating seniors. I started college in the fall. UOG was affordable for those of us who wanted to pursue a degree in the field of choice. I liked my professors and learned much from them. The campus was decent. The field house was not part of the campus yet. I spent a lot of time in the Fine Arts building studying and also in the library (RFK at the time).

In the 70's, laundromats were springing up around the island. I spent a lot of time in those establishments.

After typhoon Pamela (1976), they gave us vouchers to Town House Shopping Center.

Maureen Ann Cruz Lujan
Yigo, Guam

Memories from my mother-in-law

Dolores Jeannette Quintanilla Quinene

My grandparents sold bbq plates at the carnival – the family came to help build the shed. At the carnival you could find fiesta food including kelaguen. People also sold seafood. There was cotton candy. We had the ferris wheel there at that time too.

I helped my grandma make empanåda and boñelos to take to the schools and sell them.

We used to catch shrimp in the baçk yard, in the saddok (river).

Our family had small refrigerators, so we couldn't store much food in there.

We helped the liberation girl candidates sell tickets.

There wasn't much crime, even though we had village gangs: Barrigada vs. Agat.

During Typhoon Karen, my grandfather's house looked like it was breathing. So, we packed everybody into the car and drove to the elementary school. We were sitting on top of each other. My cousin said, *"Jeannette, we don't have to go to school tomorrow."* I said, *"Never mind school. I don't want to die!"* As we were driving away, I saw the house explode - you know how you throw a matchbox up in the air - the house blew away like that.

I remember it was a nice day that day. It was very sunny and calm. I didn't hear the animals or the birds. The palm trees were not even swaying.

A few months after the typhoon, we had a fandångo – it was the day JFK was assassinated. He's the first president I remember because he was so handsome. Even after the typhoon, I still had to starch clothes. My uncle would not wear his jeans unless it was starched.

The CB's *(construction battalion)* would come around and distribute sea rations. They built a tent city by the water – we stayed there for almost two years. It was called tent city because the roof of our house was canvas.

Dolores Jeannette Quintanilla Quinene
Originally from Agat
Currently residing in Holly Springs, NC

Memoirs of TC Dailey, US Navy

While in the US Navy, I received orders to Guam in September of 1967. I remember arriving at Anderson AFB at about 9 o'clock at night. In those days, the road from Anderson to Finegayen (NCS) was pretty doggone dark. All of the stories I'd read over the years, about WW-II and the horrific battles there came alive, as strange smells and sounds assaulted my senses. I was driven there in a pick-up truck, which gave the initial sense that things on the island were STILL a lot more primitive (unspoiled) than they really were.

The oppressive heat and humidity hit me like a brick. I'd grown up in Kansas, on a farm, so heat and humidity were not new to me, but arriving just shy of New Year's Day…well, coming from 50 degree F temperatures in San Francisco, to 89 degrees F on Guam…that was a shock. I recall that I checked in on the base, was assigned a bunk in an open-bay barracks, and then walked over to the Enlisted Men's Club (I was an E5) for a bite to eat. The sounds of the jungle were a cacophony of whistles, screeches, and insect sounds. Otherwise it was just plain dark between one light to another.

I'd been assigned to the Satellite Communications Division, which was NNW of the main base, and pretty much out there by itself. Right behind the installation was the jungle, a road, or walking trail, actually. It went from the site, all the way back to the "main-side" of the base, so it was possible to walk to and from "work" without taking the usual transport bus or somebody's car. More than once, I heard feral pigs out there, rooting about the coconut trees for copra. We avoided'em, as they could be pretty dangerous if angered.

I recall the abundance of toads and shrews – by gosh, there were MILLIONS of 'em. They'd get into everything, including one piece of SATCOM equipment we were trying out. The shrews LOVED to climb into the high voltage power units under the antenna to build nests. All went well until they got across the very high voltage, then they'd cook themselves, and ruin yet another output tube, not to mention the resulting fire from their grass and straw nests (which caught fire from the sparks). We became very proficient with the BB pistol – one needed to keep occupied, you know.

When I first got to the island, a few of my friends and I decided to make the "boonie stomp" to Talafofo Falls (we didn't quite make it). Along the way, as we were NEWBIES, we didn't bring enough water and soon we grew thirsty. Well, there were all these coconuts. From survival training, we knew that the green ones were full of water, and were NOT likely to produce the "diuretic" effect akin to a nuclear bomb. However, every time we began to cut some open, we got chased by wild pigs. They were running toward us, snorting and showing their tusks. After several of these attempts to open some coconuts without being attacked by pigs, we ran into a farmer living in the jungle in a tiny, little, tin-roofed hut. He was laughing his head off at us! Turned out, he fed his pigs copra, and the reason they ran toward us, was that they thought it was DINNER TIME!

About a month later, my car arrived from stateside. It was an old Austin-Healey "bug-eye" Sprite sports car, and well on its way to becoming a "Guam Bomb," except for not being rusty. Sprites were renowned for being untrustworthy and having a fiendish top, which two men and a boy needed to "erect" as the owner's manual so brightly put it. It was NOT a convertible, rather a "roadster." You had to stretch the top over this hellish frame that kept pulling apart, usually DURING a rainstorm. Most of the time I just left it down and dealt with the rain. GovGuam cops found it hilarious to pull up next to me in downtown Agana, waiting for a light (during a pouring rain) with my goggles on, the tonneau cover pulled up over my head (there was a "hump" in it, to clear the steering wheel). I got soaked anyways.

That silly car and I went everywhere: around the island to Merizo, Umatac, Inarajan, and Marbo. Heck, I even drove it through jungles with friends perched all over it! It beat walking! See, I remember when the Inarajan pools DID NOT have man-made sides and walkways, much less a diving board. I came to know an old farmer who lived inland from Talofofo. I fixed his old radio so I was welcomed in his squalid hut, there in the jungle. He raised pigs, who responded to the sound of a machete (Collins brand, of course) chopping coconuts. They knew it was dinner time. I'd take old clothes and beer. He and I would cook some roast pork, sometimes with some fresh-caught fish. We would sit around his hut, drinking a beer or two. He would tell me stories of "the old days" when he hid out from the Japanese, as he'd known Father Dueñas (whom they killed). He also knew of Tweed, and didn't have much good to say about him – but that's another story.

I had a girlfriend who lived just North of Inarajan, Caroline Holt. She used to sing for the Red Cross folks. Occasionally, she would sing at Governor Guerrero's house. Wow, that was quite an honor to rub elbows with the rich folks...the Joneses, Guerreros, Lujans, and all the rest. I sang in the RC coffee-house on occasion, so at least I had something out of the ordinary to offer.

The barracks I lived in were cleaned by some young girls, one of whom was called "Sissy." She was descended from the Native Chamorro people. She was very sweet and polite. One time, she invited me to her family's house. I seemed to recall it was somewhere near either Umatac or toward Cetti. They were very kind, polite, and simple folks who loved to laugh. I was always careful to be on my best behavior and manner. I think they appreciated it (too many sailors acted like idiots and behaved very rudely). Sissy made me a necklace that looked like cowries, but were a kind of seed or bean. I still have the necklace to this day. I never got to say goodbye to her....so Håfa Adai Sissy!

I was stationed at the US Naval Communications Station – Finegayan. We were pretty close to the water (wasn't everybody – nobody was further than 4 miles, although I met a family in Sinajana that had NEVER seen the ocean.....honest!). One of our favorites was Haputo Cave (better known to us as "Bare Assed Beach"). It was about a mile due NW of NCS, and down a cliff. My buddy kept his "foldboat" down there. We'd spend whole weekends at the cave / beach. It wasn't that remote, but seemingly not many went to that area. So, we usually had it to ourselves (and the little beach crabs).

I have one of those "Seagrams & Adventure" stories about it. There were mysterious piles of rocks out on the reef, just sitting there in the middle of nothing. One time, I stuck a 6-pack of Mountain Dew in the rocks. When I came back to get it, I luckily looked inside FIRST. There was a rather large morey eel inside, staring at me, who looked pretty unwilling to give up that brace of canned pop. TO THIS DAY, there is a 6-pack of MD, just waiting for somebody to go get it.

Agaña in those early days was still "mom 'n pop" with Mr. Lujan's "store" (actually a tarpaper shack on the inland side of Marine Drive) next to the boat-docks. I bought my first genuine "Collins Machete" (legitimus, it said on the blade) from him. Down the road was J&G Motors (heck, EVERYTHING was J&G something-or-other!). My favorite store, Eileen Kershaw, was the closest thing to Nordstrum store on the whole of Guam. It always smelled so good. There was always something in there of finery or class. I still have a box of incense that I purchased at Eileen's.

There was a drive-in, the name of which I can't recall. But, I once parked my bug-eye Sprite under a light pole there. When I came back with my order, the whole car was full of swarming termites! I stuck my food under the seat, as best I could, and proceeded to drive like hell toward Piti…with a trail of termites sailing out of my car like a reverse tornado. Speaking of Piti, I had a guy who worked for me, named Steve Vizzini. Steve was from LA and quite a character. He turned me on to Jimi Hendrix and Frank Zappa. He and his friends had this run-down "apartment" about 4 house-rows back from Marine Drive. The apartment was on the backside of the building. One night, with a typhoon about a week out, the wind blew the back wall OFF OF THE PLACE! It was like a 1920's movie, with the sink and toilet just hanging there by the pipes. There was nothing for a back wall except AIR and the view. It was pretty hilarious. We managed to find some rotten rope. Using the attendant palm trees for leverage, we pulled the wall back up and tied off the ropes. I wonder how long those ropes lasted before the wall fell off, surprising the hell out of somebody again.

Did you ever dive Marbo Cave? We waterproofed some Navy "battle lanterns" and did. It was just snorkeling / free-diving (no tanks). If you went into that TOTALLY CLEAR water (which WAS fresh water by the way), you'd dive down about 20 feet, then go UNDER an underwater bridge, into a back chamber that was totally dark. With the lanterns, we were able to determine that the things we felt brushing by our legs were bright-blue, fresh-water shrimp! We captured several handfuls, put'em in a net bag, and then swam out. Going down the rough & dangerous razor-sharp edges of volcanic "beach", we found some sandy beach, built a fire and roasted the shrimp in some coconut juice…..Lordy, were they good.

I later heard that Marbo Cave was where some Japanese used to get their fresh water.

Oh…and I HAVE seen taotaomona, no lie, driving back to base one night from Inarajan in my Austin-Healy 3000 (a later and much prettier car that I bought from a Navy doctor). It was on the level part that goes THROUGH the jungle, just before you get to the Talofofo Bay corners that go downhill to the bay itself. I thought I saw somebody waving in my high intensity driving lights (protection against carabao). Thinking they were stranded or lost, I pulled over, but no one was there. Then, I looked INTO the jungle. I smelled jasmine that was everywhere at once. I saw this pale, ghostly, whitish-blue figure, waving me into the jungle. I turned out the car lights, but left it running. The thing got closer, and I got scared. I jumped in the car, turned on the SUN lights, and drove like hell out of there. Later on, I told Sissy's parents. Her grandfather just shook his head in agreement. He took my hand and said, "Nothing bad will happen to you Dailey (he always called me by my last name). The taotaomona has chosen you!"

And you know what? He was right. In spite of my second visit to Vietnam, I came home intact when so many others did NOT!

My favorite haunt was at the Cliff Hotel. It was where all the Pan Am pilots and stewardesses (they called 'em back then) stayed and partied. I had saved up some money, put on my nice suit, and drove down there in my "big healey." I had a nice bite to eat, shot the breeze with the crew folks, and sometimes talked a young lady into driving around the island in my lovely red sports car. It was my big treat and a chance to act like a big shot for a while.

There are a multitude of stories I have in my head (and heart). I had some of the greatest times of my life and some of the most heart-rending, too. I watched the fully-laden bomb trucks go up to Anderson AFB (to fill the B-52s) in the afternoon and watched the MedEvac ambulance busses drive past the other way. The MedEvacs were on their way to the US Naval Hospital carrying wounded guys from Vietnam. It tore your heart out!

One of my hobbies is ham radio (Amateur Radio). I was a member of the radio club on NCS. Our call sign was KG6AAY "All American Yankee." We ran literally THOUSANDS of "phone patches" from military members to their families stateside (interfacing the phone and radio gear was called a phone patch). During the Vietnam War, we would "patch" sailors, marines, airmen, soldiers, coast guardsmen, and other folks, to mainland stations who would call them on the telephone. We ran literally THOUSANDS of them over the years. We kept lots of folks in touch with their loved ones. The most heart warming were many young marines, wounded in combat, who were able to talk to their parents, girlfriends, and wives, to tell them they were okay, that they were coming home. That made it all worth it! To hear a mom, dad, sister, brother, or girlfriend's excitement when hearing their relative's voice, over the radio, was pretty cool. We'd run them in the morning, every noon-time, and in the evening. Officers, enlisted, civilian, it didn't matter. In the "ham-shack" everybody was equal. My call-sign today is still W0EAJ (0 is a zero). You can see me as I am today at www.qrz.com/w0eaj.

August of 1969 found me preparing to leave the island. I had made the decision to leave the navy in spite of my several years of service. Something had gone out of it. I guess I also feared yet another return to Vietnam. I drove my car down to the commercial docks for transport to Oakland, CA, with a triple coat of wax on it. I left my "baby" to the "animal miscreants" who worked at the docks down by Polaris Point. That fateful morning, I rode a common bus up to Anderson – no pickup ride through the dark, steaming jungle, no mysterious arrival at a dark, forbidding place. I was just another schmuck at the terminal at Anderson waiting for the "Freedom Bird" back to "The Mystic Land of CONUS."

As I headed out to the apron, there to board a C-141 Starlifter, I saw the sign in the Anderson terminal. Like many countless other signs on military bases, it ended with the understated admonition. It read: "GUAM IS GOOD…..by order of the Commanding Officer."

Hafa Adai….dio esta Duva,

Tom Dailey
Denver, Colorado

I remember...

I remember Guam. How well I remember. It was a beautiful time in my life. I was stationed there as a young marine. I had the pleasure and honor of working for Captain Vicente Blaz, now known as Ben Blaz. I was there from 1959 to 1961 stationed at Marine Barracks, Apra Harbor. I even got to work for a short time at the Guam Daily News as a linotype operator.

I remember my pride in finishing the 75 mile hike around Guam in 55 hours. It was a hard hike, but I made it, even though some of my fellow marines had to drop out. It was quite a hike and a good way to see the perimeter of Guam. I spent many weekends on liberty in Agaña, talking with citizens of Guam and hoping to meet a pretty girl. I didn't get a chance to date any of Guam's beautiful women, but I did have the pleasure of meeting Ms. Lucy Borja. She was a good friend.

I went back to Guam in 1996 as a finalist for president of the University of Guam. I did not get the job, but I did have the opportunity of seeing Ben Blaz again and driving around the island. It had changed so much since 1961. There were all sorts of beautiful resort hotels. The beaches were crowded. Guam also has a beautiful international airport.

I still wish I could live on Guam. It's the one tropical paradise I remember so vividly.

John Garmon
Berkeley, California

I remember...

I was born on Guam and lived there until the age of ten (my father was in the Navy Civil Service). We lived in Apra Heights. I attended St. John's and Harry S. Truman Elementary School. I haven't been back since we moved, but I have fond memories of my time on the island.

The thing I remember most about Guam is the beauty of the island. Although we lived in a navy house in Apra Heights, we had coconut trees, banana trees, and hibiscus growing in our yard. Mount Lamlam was visible from our house. I can remember times it would catch on fire. My brother would have to get on top of our house to hose down the roof.

A few blocks from our house was a 1960's version of today's strip center. It had a post office, beauty shop, small grocery store, and an outdoor movie theater. We would walk to the theater at night. We'd sit outside watching the movie. This is the only outdoor theater, other than a drive in, I've ever seen.

I also remember the friendliness of the Guamanian people. When I was five or six, we were showing some visitors around the island when we came upon a fiesta at the beach. Although we didn't know any of the people, they invited us to join the festivities. The reason this memory is so vivid is because there was a cooked fish on a platter. Its head was still attached!

Margaret (Brown) McNeil
Germantown, TN

Paula's Note: Funny, when I first came to the states, I was looking for some shrimp to make kådon uhang (shrimp in coconut milk). I spent many a days looking for shrimp with the HEAD still attached. I had never known raw shrimp without a head till I came to the states.

I remember...

I remember every Thanksgiving holiday, residences of our village will lay out food and refreshments for whomever wanted to stop by and eat, drink or just shoot the bull. As I recalled, that's how I made friends with people from the southern part of Guam.

I also miss those mom and pop taverns where you are not asked for your ID to buy beer. I miss sleeping in the huts by the beaches after a night out with my friends. I miss the sound of ocean waves. I left Guam in 1966 and haven't been back since. I'm hopeful my wife and I, along with my boyhood friend, Ben Jinja, and his wife, will be going there next Spring.

Jesus Robert Cruz
Originally from Agaña Heights
Currently residing in Cedar Park, Texas

I remember…

The one thing I remember most about Guam is the Christmas season. The neighborhood kids would get together at each other's houses during nobenas. As young as we were in those days, we did not know how to answer back the Chamorro prayer responses. However, when it came to singing Fanmåtto (O Come All Ye Faithful), OMG, we could sing as loud as our heart's desired, smiling, and smirking to each other to see who could sing the loudest. After the nobena, we would gather around the table to enjoy the sweets and goodies that my mom / aunties made. Then, on to the other houses we would go.

I also remember the fiestas. Aunties, uncles, and cousins would gather early in the morning to help out with the food: bbqing the chicken for kelaguen, chopping the onions, etc. The kids, well, we would be shoved off from the outside kitchen. We were told to stay out because we were in the way. We were just curious about what was being cooked. We wanted to try the food!

I definitely remember Cool Spot!!!! Nobody, and I mean nobody, from McDonalds to Burger King, could beat the BIG BOY BURGERS!!! Yum, yum, yum!

How it all just seems like yesteryears! No place like home! I LOVE GUAM!

Odilia Sablan Cruz Ayo
Originally from Mangilao, Guam
Currently residing in Harmon, Guam

I remember...

The one thing that I thought was always cultural and a lot of fun was building the påla-påla *(military parachutes – used as tents)* for all kinds of parties. I also remember weaving the coconut leaves, making little birds, flowers, and stars to hang on the hut. We used bamboo to decorate the sides of the påla-påla and the bar. Now, that's what I call a party! It was even cooler than these tarp canopies we use these days. We used benches made of bamboo for chairs. Chamorro people are creative, some of us just got lazy and too modern too fast.

Albert & Eva Mediola
Class of 1968
Currently residing on Guam

I remember...

I vividly remember Guam because that was where I graduated junior high school in Agat and high school at JFK. Most importantly, that was where we formed Filipino bands during our high school days in the mid 1960's. Such bands were the Ambassadors, the Jaguars, New Breed, Psychotic Illusions and the Remains. Our house was in Piti Kaiser Housing. It is still there. We had moved to Guam in 1965. Three of my brothers still live on Guam. Some of our friends are still working there. We constantly communicate with them via the internet.

Ben Yanto
Manila, Philippines
Indiana, USA

The 1970's

In the 1970's…..

- **March 1972** – Bank of Guam is founded by Jesus S. Leon Guerrero. It was officially chartered on March 13, 1972. *(Bank of Guam)*
- Guam realizes the ecologic disaster caused by the brown tree snake. *(Wikipedia)*
- **April 1972** – Sergeant Yokoi, the WWII straggler is captured. He had been hiding in a cave since the war ended. *(Sanchez, pg. 405)*
- **May 21, 1976** – Super Typhoon Pamela hits Guam with sustained winds of 140 mph. *(Wikipedia)*
- **1979** – Kimberly Santos was second runner up, then crowned Miss World 1980. *(Sanchez, pg. 405)*

I remember...

We arrived in 1974 when I was eight, so my memories are colored with a kid's perspective. Every village had a patron saint and a chosen month to celebrate said patron saint with fiestas. I'm not sure how they swapped hosting duties, but someone was ALWAYS having a party. As in most areas in Polynesia (or in this case, Micronesia, but let's not split tropical hairs), a big part of the culture seems to be generosity. Back in those days (folks tell me it's different now), any stranger was welcome to walk in and share the bounty.

It would go something like this: My incredibly beautiful, blonde, haole (white person) mom would get an invitation from some random person to a fiesta. My mom, my brother (age six), and I would show up and be welcomed like royalty. I remember hearing something about strangers being considered good luck.

THE FOOD! The food was an amazing combo of the island culture....Guamanian / Chamorro, Spanish, and Filipino food.

Favorites of mine:

Bistek – some sort of marinated, thinly sliced steak.

Kelaguen – of all sorts of meat: chicken, beef & spam being my favorites. Kelaguen was cool because we got to help shred the coconut. Imagine sitting astride a wooden sawhorse with a rusty grater (a rod with a bent-up sharp end to open the coconut) and a flat, round serrated end. The kids would do this for hours to get enough coconut for everyone. I remember the meat being "raw" (only partially cooked and then cooked with vinegar…but I could be wrong).

Red rice – always!

Chicken adobo – the BEST chicken I have ever had in my life.

Corn soup – with THICK corn tortillas. I've never been able to figure out those ½ inch thick corn tortillas. They had grill marks on them.

Lumpia – the Filipino folks said this was a Filipino recipe, tiny little spring roll-esque fried bits of heaven. A pain to make, but SO, SO, SO, yummy. Actually, verging on addictive.

Pancit – another "Pilipino Pood" (so our friends described it). Very yummy noodle dish – not sure if they're buckwheat? But, the texture was very different. I remember chicken and celery with fresh lemon flavors.

Fina'denne sauce – with tiny red peppers….HOT and to be added with everything.

Pickled green papaya – HOT, HOT, HOT, and addictive. Kids would bring baggies of these to sell at the bake sales.

Roast pork – we had neighbors with pigs, and I stumbled across them slaughtering a pig for a fiesta. I didn't get to see much, but I saw it hanging so the blood could drain.

The adults would all chew betelnut by making a little pouch of pupulu leaves and filling it with the SUPER bitter nut and some limestone. I tasted it once and WOW. I spit it right out. Everyone laughed at the little haole girl with her white hair…..

Whitney Dickinson

The above was reprinted with permission from Whitney. This was her entry on foodchains.blogspot.com.

I remember…

I remember the weddings! Oh! My mother had eight brothers. So, as you know Chamorro traditions, the groom / groom's family gets all the bridal things together. I remember the wedding gowns, jewelry, shoes….everything the bride had to wear on her special day. It was all laid in this big trunk. I remember walking up to the bride's house. People were playing music, singing, dancing. Drinks were brought in as well. The bride had another gown she wore that Friday night. Come Saturday was the wedding at the church. We would go to the bride's house for the breakfast party and then the groom's house later in the evening. That is all gone now. Everything is so fast paced. Jeez! You can go to a wedding drive thru out in Vegas. Hopefully, someday, someone will bring the wedding traditions back. I guess I'm a bit of a romantic.

Lynn Atoigue
Originally from Talofofo
Currently residing in Honolulu, Hawaii

I remember...

I remember the variety of cultural expectations placed upon me, especially as a returning-to-home military brat. Most traditions and customs were foreign to me and my siblings. Luckily, both of my parents were from Inarajan where we were surrounded by fellow Chamorros and extended family members. This enabled me to learn my language and my customs, as opposed to being greatly westernized. I did not forget what it meant to be a Chamorro. I learned to converse in Chamorro simply by interacting with relatives and friends that were around me in my village.

In the late 1970's, I was hired as the youth center supervisor of the Inarajan rec center. This center was the focal point of many Inarajan residents. Sadly, I witnessed that with the advent of cable T.V., there was a stark decline of residents who patronized our facility. Attendance at activities such as monthly dances and sporting events became sparse. Residents seemed to opt to stay within their homes to watch T.V. I long to see once again people congregating at the village recreation center, thus influencing and fostering a sense of family....which seems to be sadly drifting away.

Blaine Flores Afaisen
Originally from Inarajan
Currently residing in Perris, California

I remember…

My first introduction to Guam was as a fledgling exotic dancer. I had been working in Honolulu when my agent suggested a booking on Guam. Not being very sound in my geography, I thought that this island was one of the small, unknown places in Hawaii! After what seemed like a very long plane trip, I found myself peering down at a lovely oasis in the early morning of 1975. I was smitten and destined to return many times with great happiness.

Thru Typhoon Pamela, baby lifts, Navy mishaps, potholes, Club Yobo, duty buses, runaway hotdog carts, fiestas, incredible hospitality, and a tree full of resting monarch butterflies, my heart is full to have had the Chamorro experiences. Guam is a beautiful island made up of very kind, loving people! I am so incredibly grateful.

With best wishes to all and Spam in my heart…

Judith Stein

I remember…

I was lost in the jungle on Guam in 1971 or 1972. I remember the headline of the newspaper, "Busy Day for Guam Police as Four Die and Two Lost in Jungle." There was a bad car crash that day, too, where four people had died. My dad was in the navy at NAS Agaña.

I remember Sgt. Yokoi coming out of the jungle when I lived there as a kid. I remember a plane catching fire and burning on the runway at the air station. Mostly, I remember how much fun I had there as a kid. I had fun too when I came back while enlisted in the navy myself. I was stationed at the northern end of the island at the communications station and the old Navfac.

Valerie Lovelace
Poland, Maine

The 1980's

In the 1980's…..

- The Guam Rail or Ko'ko' is extirpated (local extinction) from the entire island of Guam by the late 1980s. The decline in Guam's bird population, to include the ko'ko' comes after the unintentional introduction of the brown tree snake. Currently, the ko'ko' is being bred in captivity on Guam and a few mainland U.S. zoos. *(Wikipedia)*
- CASAMAR Guam was established in 1980 – fishing fleet sales & services. CASAMAR is located in Apra Harbor within the Commercial Port of Guam. They also service military ships and other marine vessels. *(Casamar)*

Memories from my brother

Paul Edward Lujan Jr.

I remember spearfishing up north at Ritidian Point. When I was in middle school, I used to walk the sand and follow the flashlights while dad spearfished with his friends. Those days, it wasn't illegal to fish there, all you had to do was get a military sponsor. The fish were so huge back then, even the kichu and seyon were caught from 7 to 10 inches. After years of following my dad and his friends fishing, I finally got to do it myself when my dad retired his fins. He didn't know that I was using his equipment, well, that's what I thought before. I'd spend the whole day out there learning the channel and the cuts and holes from Ritidian to Scout beach. The reef that way was amazing and dangerously tricky. In high school, I remember taking some of the football "SHARKS" guys out there to spear. In fact, my friend, a haole dude named Ben Whitaker, got into it. I couldn't go spearfishing one day so I let him borrow my gear. I was worried because the water up there was extremely dangerous if you didn't know the tide and the current. He went out at daytime and he came back about 7 p.m. I couldn't believe the size and amount he caught.

I had a lot of good times up that way fishing with many of my friends: Juls, Ralph, Ron, Mike, Chach, JR, Bob, Ken, Pat, Joey, Jerry, Jaret, Justin. It would be nice if things were the way they were before. Most good fishing spots are preserved now. Spear-fishing was life for me back in Guam, but it got harder to do. The last time I spear-fished, I ended up in the back of a Guam police car. HaHa! I never got my spear-gun back! The officers at the station had a good lobster and fish dinner! GOOD TIMES! GOOD FISHING! GOOD MEMORIES!

Paul E. Lujan, Jr.
Originally from Yigo, Guam
Currently residing in Holly Springs, NC

Paula's Note: My brother and I, along with our siblings and the rest of our neighborhood friends, truly were blessed to have had each other growing up! We were lucky to have had so many kids in our area of GHURA 506. The first ten boys my brother mentioned above were our direct neighbors. Most of our parents / families still live there! Our lives were not perfect, but I am sure it was that very environment that gives us someplace to go home to, so to speak!

My family moved there in 1980. I wish I could give my children that same environment! Life is different here in the mainland. It is my hope, at least with my books, that I can somehow share that life not only with my kids and your kids, but with their descendants!

I remember...

I was stationed on Guam (Anderson AFB) from January 1981 to April 1982. I was naturalized in Agaña. I loved the island, but I think more so now than back then. Every time I drove around it and explored I found something new to photograph. I can honestly say it is the most beautiful place I ever lived. The memory that sticks out the most in my mind is Christmas on the beach. We had a Santa, but he had shorts on. We all did. It was nice. I miss the fiestas, too. I remember Tumon Bay. It was awesome at night. My favorite part of the island was down at the southern end on the Pacific side. There were several parks along the shore. I need to go dig out some pictures. I'm "homesick" now.

Pete Goodwin
Indiana University Cyclotron Facility

I remember...

What do I remember about Guam? I met my wife while living there. That was over 17 years ago. We got married at the Governor's mansion, by Gov. Paul Ada. I remember everything about that island. The weather was perfect everyday. The island food at the fiestas is something I still can't make or find anywhere. The beaches were amazing as was the scuba diving. The night life was awesome. The locals were very cool. I lived there for two years ('88-'90) and have missed it everyday. There is no way to say anymore with this limited space, so I'll end. But, I WILL be back...to the "rock."

John R. White

I remember...

The one thing that stood out the most for me was the "FIESTAS". The word itself is like a magnet. It attracts people from all over the island to enjoy authentic Chamorro dishes, music, and socialization. Thank you for allowing others like me to contribute to something very important to our people. It is individuals like you that continue to keep our culture strong.

Annie S. Tyquingco
Originally from Malesso (Merizo)
Killeen, Texas

I remember...

I was born on Guam, but I'm Filipino. I went to school at Simon Sanchez High School. I was the fourth child out of seven living in Yigo. We had a relaxing time when we went to Ypao Beach during the heat of summer. When it was too hot, we went to the mall. Everyone knew everyone.

When I wanted to shop for bargains, we would go to Town House or Ben Franklin. My dad's favorite past time was going to the Flea Market on Saturdays.

I was in the honor band at Sanchez. We marched in the parade. It was a neat experience for me. We did get sunburned, but it was fun. Sanchez was a fun school.

Every village had a fiesta. It was so much fun. There were tons of food and fun music to dance to, especially the cha-cha, which was my favorite. Growing up on Guam was simple, innocent, and fun.

I was a mostly quiet student. My parents were strict with me and didn't make me go out so much. All the events and simple fun added up to the great memories I had and shared with friends at Simon Sanchez.

Shirley Torres Offhaus
Originally from Yigo, Guam
Currently residing in Washington, D.C.

I remember...

I lived on Guam from January 1979 to May 1982. My dad was stationed at Naval Station. We lived in military housing, surrounded by civilian housing. The Marine barracks was just a stone's throw away. Guam and the Navy are forever linked in my head.

I attended New Piti Elementary School in sundresses and flip-flops. I remember as well that creepy military cemetery across the street and the tropical jungle all around. I remember the long bus-drive in which the bus-driver would go out of his way to pick up students far up in the mountains: the high-walled jungle on one side, the sheer drop to the Pacific Ocean on the other. I remember Brownie Fun Day at Anderson Air Force Base (it seems as if the entire island's worth of Girl Scout Brownies attended this event).

Coconut trees grew in our front yard. My mom, several months pregnant, climbed up with a machete in her mouth because she had a craving for coconut. I remember pulling star apples fresh from a neighbor's tree. I thought real apples were weird and exotic.

My mom was always surrounded by other navy wives. The kids would come and go throughout each others' houses as if they lived there. I remember the countless outdoor bbq parties, including one neighbor across the street whom seemed to have one EVERYDAY, and everyone was invited.

I remember going with my family to Gab-Gab Beach for weekend beach parties. I saw my first octopus there. I remember my father sneaking onto Gab-Gab at night to do some night-fishing. I woke up to see live fish and octopi in the kitchen sink.

We made bookmarks, mats, and hats from palm leaves. I remember watching the sixth graders put together a real Chamorro hut in the school yard for Magellan's Day.

We took a field trip to an authentic Chamorro village. I think it was actually for tourists, but hey, I was only seven or eight years old, so what did I know at the time? I remember eating coconut candy, getting coconut soap, and riding my first (and only) water buffalo.

I knew the Chamorro language (taught in schools) much better than my parents' own language (Ilocano). I remember dancing a traditional Chamorro dance at the school talent show. The dance involved brooms and a handful of little barefoot girls in traditional dress.

I remember so many things about Guam. Even though I was ten years old when my family left, over twenty-six years ago, I still consider Guam my childhood home. My father was transferred to Dallas, Texas. My entire family and I still live in North Texas. I could go on and on, but I think this is enough for your collection. Thank you for doing this!

Rufel Ramos

I remember...

I was in the U.S. Air Force. I remember Tarague Beach. I went there every weekend and played volleyball all day long. I remember Typhoon Roy washed the beach onto the road. When I first got there, my friends and I went snorkeling a lot at Gabgab Beach and Piti Bomb Hole. We bought the cheapest snorkeling equipment we could find.

Gary Moczulski, Holly Springs, NC.....our neighbor

The 1990's

In the 1990's…..

- **August 28, 1992** – Super Typhoon Omar passed over Guam reaching up to 115 mph winds. Omar brought heavy rains, flooding Guam with almost a foot of water. Additionally, an "astronomical high tide" occurred increasing the damage brought on by Omar. *(Wikipedia)*
- **August 8, 1993** – an 8.1 earthquake rocks Guam. Do you remember? *Paula's Note: I was there. I remember the dishes wouldn't stop rattling, the ground kept moving. Typical earthquakes on Guam were but a few seconds. This one seemed to go on forever.*
- **December 16, 1997** – Super Typhoon Paka blows over Guam with winds at 145 mph, gusting from 171-184 mph. *(Wikipedia)*

Memories from my sister
Pearl Amber Lujan Ungacta

I remember the drive to my Grandma Cabe's house in Canada, Barrigada, Lujan Way.

I remember following my Grandma Cruz who was the techa *(someone who leads the prayer)* for someone's nobena *(a prayer gathering of family and friends)*. It was interesting to listen to how fast she could say the prayer in Chamorro, as well as how lovely she sang the songs. I remember anticipating the refreshments the families would serve after the nobena. When it was time for a nobena at Grandma Cruz's house, I remember we would always race to get a nobena book.

I watched my dad use a machete to cut open a young coconut. When he got close enough to the soft coconut shell, he would poke a hole through the shell and tell me to get a cup. He would drain the månha juice into the cup. My dad told me to never scratch the inner shell because it will affect the månha tree in some way. I enjoy my månha cold, with some sugar added. After watching my dad a few times, I learned how to do it myself, that is, when I was brave enough to face the machete! I enjoyed this quite a bit!

I remember Lost Pond quite well because I went there several times with my mom, my brothers, and my cousins. It was a hidden place. We would park at NCS Beach then walk a little over a mile on the sand. When we were in view of Shark's Hole, we headed into the jungle. We walked just under a mile from that point to get to Lost Pond. Sometimes, I was scared to be there because I just didn't know what was going to jump out of the jungle. It was amazing though: the scenery of the pond itself, my brothers and cousins jumping off the rope which dangled from a tree, and swimming in that fresh, pond water. If you haven't been there, you are truly missing out! Thanks mom for taking us to Lost Pond!

I remember the food I bought: buchi-buchi at Onedera store in Dededo, empanåda at the store by Ypao Beach, Joanne's loaf of bread at Joanne's Bakery in Yigo, Spanish Gold at American Bakery, banana lumpia at Dededo Public Health from the parked canteen, sweet and sour soaked in Tabasco and vinegar, pickled mango / pickled papaya from a mom and pop store, and Assam milk tea.

I remember the things I hand-picked: iba (the yellow, tiny, sour fruit), åbas (the sweet, green fruit with lots of seeds, sometimes larger than an apple), hutu (the black nut from the dokdok tree, eaten after it has been boiled), kamachili (the fruit that looks like tamarind, but sweet and white, with black seeds), adduk (the mini, grape-like seaweed, oh so sour, but good), pahung (the nut from the pandanus bush), mansanita (the small, berry like fruit that has millions of seeds) mountain apple (a reddish apple, shaped like a mountain, white inside), and finally, star apple (it looks like a star when sliced) of which I enjoyed sprinkled with salt.

Pearl Lujan Ungacta
Originally from Yigo
Currently residing in Haveloc, NC

I remember...

To this day I still miss Guam. It's a small, but beautiful island. Anyone who enjoys the simple life will love it there. The ocean view is breathtaking, while the sunsets are picturesque. I miss the rooster waking me up at 5 a.m. and waiting for the chickens to cross the road, so that my car could pass.

But, if you like the big city, there's a section where you can shop the well known stores and eat in famous restaurants. I, personally, like the sushi bars! I was surprised that Guam has so many of the fast food eateries that we have here in New York, everything from McDonalds to Taco Bell to Pizza Hut to Kentucky Fried Chicken! You name it, Guam has it!

At first, the humidity killed me, but after a month my body adapted to it. Besides, every place you go to has air conditioning or air con, as the people on the island call it.

And, let's not forget the people. They are so friendly. They go out of their way to please and accommodate you. I actually became acquainted with people who will be lifetime friends. My only regret is not being able to visit them regularly.

My memories of Guam will last a lifetime!

Lynn Perlongo
New York City

I remember...

I was on Guam from October 1992 to October 1994. I was in the U.S. Navy and worked on Naval Station Port Ops on the tugboats. I just loved being on the island and its laid back ways. I had a good time going places around the island and learning about them. The people were ever so friendly. The civilians I worked with during that time were great: Frank, Bill, and the crew. I have lots of memories of Guam and lots of pictures I took as I drove around the island. When I can afford to, I want to take my daughter there to visit and to see Guam. When people ask me what Guam was like, I tell them Guam was wonderful. They enjoy the pictures I have to show them. So, thanks for the memories!

Elizabeth Griffiths
Silver Springs, Florida

I remember...

RELIGIOUS COMMITTMENTS
    Lent week - we were isolated from social amenities (no television, radio, playing outside, making loud noise, fighting, etc.).

    Fiestas - every village celebrating their patron saint.

Sunday Mass - I remember mass as a social gathering as well as a day to give praise and thanks to the Lord.

ECONOMY

I remember the fast food chains and local restaurants. Guam's shopping malls were expanding. The local stores, such as Hafa Adai Exchange and Bartis House, were going out of business.

SOCIAL LIFE

Family gatherings were at "Family Beach." We were allowed to play unsupervised. We had a trusting community. I remember the Hula / Tahitian performances.

EDUCATION / SPORTS

I remember the support by parents at high school sports activities. The Guam Youth Football League was a popular league during the summer. School was enforced and encouraged depending on the home situation. School was hardly diverse. There were primarily Micronesian and Filipino ethnicities.

I remember Guam with great memories. The island is enriched with culture and indulged with simplicity.

Jonilynn Reyes
Currently residing in South Carolina

Memories from a young man who spent a few childhood years on Guam

THE BEACHES

Gabgab Beach….snorkeling on through the clear water and poking sea cucumbers, watching the tiger-like fish swim by, and drops of salt water splashing on my back from the flying fish leaping over me. The porcupine fishes were nothing to mess with, but my sister used to catch them when looking for squid. The waves were not bad: strong enough to carry you back to shore on a knee board, but weak enough to swim through. It was tropical paradise with a steady breeze cooling you from the hot sun. The water was warm like a bubble bath.

THE WEATHER

Sunshine on my shoulders made me happy everyday for the most part. I loved it! Whenever it rained, the sun was usually out. We called it "golden showers." Typhoons were incredible. My family would stock up on cases of SPAM and Vienna Sausage, Hawaiian Punch, Guava Juice cans, and bags of rice. We also prepared by taping the windows. The best part was the power outages. When the eye of the storm was over us, it felt like a break from the chaos the storm brought all around.

THE BOONIES

When I first went into the boonies with my gang of friends, that wilderness felt alive: green lizards, geckos, hummingbirds, snakes, banana spiders, beautiful flowers protected by butterflies, and praying mantises. It was off limits to all at night especially children because of abduction by the taotaomonas. There were many legends about the taotaomonas. As we heard more stories about them, our awareness heightened, especially around the taotaomona trees.

THE FIESTAS

These were the biggest celebrations all over the island for birthdays, holidays, and other special occasions. There was enough food to last for days including a pig. We had so much fun: card games, karaoke, and plenty of dancing with the children running all over the place. The islanders were so friendly. My favorite food besides daigo is coconut candy. If the party was on the beach, some of the guys would swim to Cocos Island and back.

Marcus A. Ashby, Charleston, S.C.

I remember...

I remember riding with my papa in his truck to the hardware store. It always seemed like there was something that he needed there. We seemed to drive to all the stores before he finally found what he needed. We'd also stop by the little stores to grab some snacks. I LOVE Assam black tea, cheese curls, and shrimp chips. I loved those items.

I remember my kindergarten teacher, Mrs. Rose Eide. She was a cool teacher. She made me feel very good. She taught at J.Q. San Miguel Elementary School in Toto. I also remember Mrs. Antoinette Nadeau. She was my third grade teacher at J.Q. One time, when my bangs were long and it would block my view of the chalkboard, Mrs. Nadeau told me to tell my mom to cut my hair or she'll cut it herself. I didn't know if she was joking. My mom said that she couldn't do it. I cut it myself. I cut it really short. I remember Mrs. Nadeau felt so bad.

Asan Park: WOW! That was the best place to fly a kite because there weren't any power lines. For some reason, we always had a hard time getting our kites off the ground. We weren't always successful, but it was always fun. We'd have a little picnic there too.

Christmas always felt Christmasy! We'd go to church and then to one of the hotels for brunch with the whole Cruz family. There would be a lot of us. Afterwards, we'd all drive to great-grandma's house in Dededo. We would all open up our presents. It was always fun.

On my last trip to Guam in June 2007, I went with my uncle, Ben San Nicolas, to the drag strip. I got to ride with him as he raced his car. I had a lot of fun. I never got to do that ever before. Uncle Ben even let me practice driving a stick shift around his house.

I like how we were brought up to call our close cousins "brother" and "sister." I liked that. We were really close. Nonnie, Tonnie, Shanna, KC, and Toya are really my first cousins. We refer to them as my sisters. I like how family is very important on Guam. Or, how my mom's best friend from her childhood is my "auntie." Auntie Phan knew my mom and her family since she was young. She is Chinese. I was confused as to how she could be my auntie.

Sean-Joaquin Thornton, Fort Worth, Texas

The 2000's

2000 – present

- **2000 Census** – In 2000, Guam's population was at 154,805. In 2007, the population was estimated at 173,460. *(Wikipedia)*
- **December 8, 2002** – Super Typhoon Pongsona races over Guam with peak winds at 173 mph. Pongsona was the third most intense to hit Guam, behind only a typhoon in 1900 and Super Typhoon Karen in 1962. *(Wikipedia)*
- **Military** – Marines moving to Guam? Here are a list of Guam military bases to date: **U.S. NAVY:** U.S. Naval Base Guam at Sumay; Apra Harbor at Orote Peninsula; Ordinance Annex at Naval Magazine; Naval Computer & Telecommunications Station at Barrigada & Finegayan; **U.S. AIRFORCE:** Andersen Air Force Base at Yigo; **U.S. COAST GUARD:** U.S. Coast Guard District 14 Sector Guam at Sumay; **GUAM NATIONAL GUARD:** Joint Forces Headquarters Guam at Radio Barrigada and Fort Juan Muna. Total land area occupied by military is 39,000 acres or 29%. *(Wikipedia)*

I remember...

It's only been five and a half years since I left our home, the beautiful island of Guam. I remember the beautiful people and their hospitality, the beautiful, preserved southern part of Guam, the outings "at the ranch," the barbeques, and the beach outings.

I could never erase the memory of being at the Cathedral in Agaña and most especially St. Jude Thaddeus in Sinajana, the parish I grew up in. It could be twenty years, and the images will still be vivid in my memory!

I love and miss my home, the beautiful island of Guam! I hope to move back some day!

Monica M. Mendiola, 34 years old
Currently residing in Tacoma, Washington

I remember...

I was on Guam during the summer of 2003. I stayed at Uncle Tony and Auntie Mary's house in Barrigada Heights. I remember Uncle Tony killing a chicken.

I liked sightseeing on Guam. We went to the convent. I loved all of the flowers. I hung out with Nikki, Johnny, and Marianna Cabe.

I also went to the convent with Sister Monica. She is my godmother and Uncle Tony's oldest sister. I also met Archbishop Arroyo on Guam.

Katie Roberts
Concord, NC

I remember...

My dad was in the Air Force stationed on Guam. I was sixteen years old. I remember the beautiful beaches and hanging out with Nikki Cabe. I remember the culture and the people.

Stefanie Ancheta

This year or that

Memories from my sister-in-law

Colleen M. Borreta Garrido

I remember being at my family's favorite beach, USO. I remember going home, sitting in the back of my dad's truck, looking at the sunset, and feeling the warm breeze. One of my favorite places in the world is the village I grew up in, Tamuning. Every time I visit Guam, the streets, the houses, and the people are still there. I remember my family preparing for a big feast: the men killing the pig and standing by the barbeque pit while the ladies were in the house cooking. I always look forward to the sunset and the cool breeze at night when I am on Guam.

Colleen M. Borreta Garrido
Hawaii

I remember...

First of all, thank you for giving me the opportunity to share what I remember about Guam. It really means a lot to me.

What stood out for me from my five years spent on Guam are the people. I have never met anyone who holds a candle to the Chamorro people. I learned so much while I was there. I was fortunate enough to live with a local family, so I got to experience "local life" first hand. I was also lucky enough to come away with a few recipes! YUM! You don't know how much I miss the food there!

I think the first thing I said when I came back state-side was, "you haoli people are soooo spoiled!" I really miss the relaxed atmosphere of the island, and the ethics that most of the locals held. I just wish I could have learned more of the language while I was there. My son is half Chamorro, and I wish I could teach him the language. Some day, I hope to be able to take him back to Guam, so he can see for himself how beautiful his birth place is. I'd rather he visited instead of hearing it from me or looking at pictures. Well, thank you again for your email. I hope to receive more pertaining to my "Home-away-from-Home."

Sundee Burney
Bullhead City, Arizona

I remember...

I remember going to Merizo every Sunday to visit dad's side of the family. We wanted to eat what they offered, but mom and dad said, "No" because we already ate.

The people from Rome came to the Catholic Church on Guam to relay their testimony. They had envisioned Mary. There was a big ceremony in Agana when they did a procession from Agaña to Fort Apugan. When they were at the top, there was a tsunami on Marine Drive, in front of the old Mark's Department Store.

When I went in to my appointment, the third floor of Naval Hospital, I could see the cracks on the wall. "How about we had an earthquake when I'm in labor," I said. James replied "Don't worry babe, I'll carry you out of here."

Vanessa Pangelinan
South Carolina

I remember...

People talking about Santa Maria – when they take her off-island, we have bad weather! They take her to get painted and to do her hair.

In 1976, there was a big earthquake. We had a tin house. The tin was moving as if someone took a big shovel and hit the side of the house.

James Pangelinan
South Carolina

I remember...

It was on Guam when I first witnessed the slaughtering of a pig ready to be cooked for a party. The pig squealed and squealed before its throat was slit. It was a horrific sight and sound, but very interesting for this young lad.

Jay Thornton
Fort Worth, Texas

I remember...

I remember feeding Grandpa Cabe's roosters. I ran from the brown tree snakes in grandpa's back yard. I remember working at the Hilton. It was very hot on Guam.

Deshaun Cabe
Orlando, FL

I remember...

I remember during the weekends, we had a function we had to go to. We were always around family and friends. We got to see everybody. I miss that. There was never a dull moment. I always had something to look forward to. Regardless of the occasion, people always found a way to turn it into a big party.

Nikki Cabe
North Carolina

.

I remember...

At five years old, using the old bamboo traps to catch land crab with my grandmother, using a talåya for the first time with my grandfather, and camping out at Tanguisan Beach with my grandparents and the rest of my family. I remember skinning my first lechon, how much the tångantångan hurt on my behind, and climbing the mango trees with my father. There are too many memories of my paradise home that come rushing to me, way too many to mention and speak of: carnivals in July, Coconut Olympics, etc. Life on Guam was true paradise. It was true life. Growing up on Guam as a child, we were able to enjoy the beautiful beaches and natural landscape. That was then, this is now. Hotels seem to block everything that was: beaches such as Sirena Beach, Gun Beach, Ypao Beach, Matapang Beach. All are now gone. All that are built in their places are permanent blemishes on my once cherished playground.

The island is still a very beautiful place. I do cherish every visit to my home. Still, I am saddened by what I see on every return visit.

Frances C. P. Quenga (VanTress)
Originally from Piti

I remember...

I went to Guam on "vacation" or to "check it out" with some friends of mine that were going there on business. When I left the states, my return date was set at ninety days. I had planned on going and staying for a while. If I didn't like it or it didn't work out for me, then I would come back a few months later. I loved Guam. I ended up living there for eight and a half years. While I was on Guam, I worked in radio for KUAM for two years, then Sorensen Pacific Broadcasting (now Sorensen Media Group) for six and a half years.

Brian Curit

I remember...

I was born and raised on Guam. I left the island when I was eighteen years old.

I remember that the concept of the "extended family" was very strong when I was growing up on Guam. I remember growing up in Tamuning with neighbors consisting of my grandparents (my dad's side), aunts, uncles, and cousins (dad's side too).

We celebrated birthdays and other holidays together. I remember that favorite family recipes were shared during each event. Some family members were known to specialize in a particular Chamorro dish. I remember when my mom and mama (grandmother on my mom's side) would always invite me to help prepare recipes by cutting and mixing ingredients. I still use the "kitchen prep" techniques that were taught by my elders.

Phyllis Arndt
Originally from Tamuning, Guam

Stories

&

Letters

A letter from John P. Rabon

Buenas yan Hafa Adai,

I received your email requesting assistance in the first edition of "Remember Guam." My name is John Perez Rabon. I was born in 1960 and have lived all my life on Guam. I was raised in the village of Barrigada (Radio Barrigada). I am the fifth of six children.

I remember most the closeness of the family back then. My grandmother (dad's mom) was living with us. After falling and breaking her hip, she was bedridden for several years before she passed away in her sleep. My mother took care of her daily feedings. I remember my grandmother using a mortar and pestle to break up the betelnut, and then combine it with the pepper leaf (pupulu) and lime stone powder (åfuk). She did this everyday.

I remember, really, only receiving two gifts (toys) every year when I was a child: one during my birthday and the other was at Christmas time. Most of our time was spent outside playing. We only had one channel back then. We didn't get cable T.V. until the 1970's. The most important time was the rosary hour on Sunday afternoons when the family would gather and pray.

My father had a ranch where we would go everyday to tend to the animals and the farm. We did everything outdoors. I fondly remember my father as a master weaver. He would weave hats, fans, baskets, and that diamond shaped container for flavored rice, the katupat.

My mom and dad were in their teens during the war. They married right after the island was re-taken. My dad (Tåta) relayed a story to me when he was with the Guam Combat Patrol. He helped the U.S. soldiers with the mop up operations, rounding up the remaining Japanese stragglers. In one story, Tåta told me that they were close to catching one very elusive straggler. They were so close, that they found his camp with a fire going and rice still cooking. Apparently, the straggler must have sensed them coming. He left in such a hurry that he forgot his sword, Japan flag, and a silver dollar. When I asked him what had happened to the sword and flag (which would have been a great keepsake), Tåta told me that he gave them away to the soldiers. When I asked why he did not keep them for himself, he looked at me and said that back then, they wanted nothing that reminded them of the Japanese and what they had done to the people. I could not imagine the horror and atrocities that had befallen him, his family, and friends. But, my father did say that he kept that silver dollar.

My father passed away in 1987. When my mother passed on in 2007, she had given me that very silver dollar which my father kept. Now, I have that 1898 silver dollar. I will pass it to my children, along with the story of how their grandfather had obtained it.

Paula, thank you for letting me share, but one of my father's stories from the war.

Sincerely,
John P. Rabon

An essay from Joshua J. Aguon

Remember Guam
Turning the pages, remembering the memories, living for the future

"Go play," my mother told me as I begged her to let me help in the kitchen. I was six years old at the time. My mother and her family owned a catering business just behind grandma's yellow, tin-roofed home in Piti. I can only envision what were great times then with a bright fluorescent sign that said, "Villagomez Catering 477-3133."

I remember stepping foot just at the base of the catering kitchen door. My cousins rode their bikes amidst the kaskahu. The hen and her young ran through the brush. The air was filled with sweet smelling cakes, hot red rice, and fried chicken – all in preparation for the night's fiesta. Each brother and sister made a particular dish. They all could cook. *It didn't matter who made each dish. At the end, the dish tasted the way it was supposed to.*

I was able to refresh my childhood memories with a little help from mom's albums and dad's video tapes. It looked like year after year, the fiestas at grandma's house kept getting larger and larger (probably because grandma's birthday fell around the same weekend as the Piti fiesta). The tape ran from morning till night. I could see all the children scattered about. My older cousins were hustling and bustling with the decorations. Uncle Albert and some others were turning the roast pig, over and over again. The band and the DJ were setting up. Grandpa was laughing. The dogs were barking. I could hear the clatter in the catering kitchen. I could see the floral arrangements being made. Finally, I saw me – looking on.

I caught a glimpse of Auntie Charo in the background wiping a tear away while the table was blessed. The tape continued with music and dancing and children and families wandering about. Then, there I was, in grandma's arms while everyone sang, "Happy Birthday to you…"

These simple memories may not be treasured by most, but they are all I have as time progresses. I come to realize Guam truly has changed, not just in infrastructure, in scenery, or in atmosphere, but in the ways we live. Just by that, it alters everything we're all about. Truly, these memories keep me grounded and entwined in the roots of my past. They are a symbolic measure for me in the future.

Joshua Justin (Villagomez) Aguon
19, UOG Student
Sinajana, Guam

The following excerpt is reprinted with permission from the author, Robert M. Blevins. This is a portion of Mr. Blevin's story, "Island Adventures With Mother."

I never understood all the details about why my mother left San Francisco and dragged me off to the Phillippines, and then later, Guam. In any event, I was a six-year-old kid, and it was a lot of fun. One minute she was a hard-working single mother typing for Betty Crocker, and the next, she suddenly booked passage for us on a freighter bound for Manila. She said my grandfather had an import-export business there, and that she was going to work for him.

The 'Franklin Pierce' took its good time wandering across the Pacific. Along the way we made stops at Kwajalein Atoll, Midway, and half the islands the Japanese occupied during World War II. One advantage to taking passage on a freighter is that you get to eat with the officers. I always minded my manners. Mother was strict on that one......

A year later, mother decided we were going to Guam. Shortly after we arrived, we met my soon-to-be-father. Larry was a civilian worker for Anderson Air Force Base and pumped jet fuel. He took us to the drive-in every weekend. I think they waited for me to fall asleep. After they married, I acquired a REAL family, since Larry had a boy and a girl from a previous marriage.

My new brother and I wandered the hills and jungles on Guam for the next few years. When we gathered all our friends and played 'Army,' we used real tanks and artillery pieces left over from the war as props. You could find spent brass everywhere. Some people collected this stuff for a while, including unexploded shells. But when a shell went off in someone's house in Apra Heights and blew the roof away, the Army Ordinance boys started cleaning up the island. It took them years! My new father bought us a plastic-molded rowboat and my new brother and I plied the lagoons as pirates until a reef finally tore out the bottom of the boat.

After a few years, an approaching typhoon gave my mother an excuse to leave the island. We moved to Seattle, where my father took a job with Boeing. We've been here ever since.

Robert M. Blevins
Seattle, WA

A Soldier's Father, A Soldier's Uncle

Dear Paula,

I was surfing the 3rd Marine Div. Assn. website. I saw your posting. I thought I'd send you a note.

My dad, Cpl. Charles G. Moore, was in the Guam campaign as was his older brother Troy Moore. Dad was with E. Company, 2nd Battalion, 3rd Marine Regiment. Uncle Troy was in C Company, 1st Battalion, 307th Infantry Regiment, 77th Infantry Division.

Uncle Troy passed away back in 1965. Dad just turned 83 on September 30, 2007. Dad went back to Guam in July 1994 for the celebration of the liberation of Guam. I wished uncle Troy could have lived long enough for that celebration.

During the war, they didn't know the whereabouts of one another because of mail censorship. But, one day, as dad's unit was moving down a coral road, he saw a soldier standing on a bank along the road where soldiers were resting. They saw each other and met in the middle of the road, hugging and crying. The marines and soldiers thought a fight was breaking out. They all ran out to get in on it when they realized that this was a joyous reunion. They all stopped and shared in the happy occasion.

Dad was at Chinito Hill where several bad fights broke out. He was wounded and sent down to the hospital or what remained of it. While there, three Japanese tanks attacked. Dad never spoke of this, but my youngest brother, who went with dad in 1994, told me that dad's oldest buddy had this to say: he (dad) almost single-handedly took out those tanks as they advanced on the hospital.

On another occasion, dad's twelve man patrol was hit by a banzai attack one night. The Japanese finally pulled out at dawn. Dad, who was the BAR man, found one guy alive and 75 dead Japanese soldiers. The one survivor, Paul Dzyak (spelling?) is still alive and living in Cleveland, Ohio. They keep in touch. Paul was cut up pretty badly with a samurai sword. That was Paul's ticket home.

When dad went back to Guam in 1994, the park service finally got him to talk on video, something we've tried to do for years. So, next time you are home, you might try them. I would have loved to have gone with him, but I was at Ft. Stewart, Georgia, out in the boonies and couldn't make it.

On his second trip to Guam, Dad said he was overwhelmed by the hospitality and generosity of the Chamorro people. He was touched by the kindness of the young people who were not even alive during WWII. If I can help you, just write and I'll try.

Semper Fi and This We'll Defend!!
David Moore

A letter to Paula, from a military mom

Dear Paula,

I just received your cookbook from Amazon.com. I am thrilled to find so many great Chamorro recipes. Let me tell you why.

My oldest son is in the US Air Force. He and his family were stationed on Guam for two years at Andersen AFB. My husband and I were fortunate enough to visit them for two weeks in June 2005. We were all from Florida originally, so we were familiar with a tropical environment. Guam is so full of beauty and history. I was so captivated with the island and the people. I decided to bring some of it home to share.

We live in Johnson City, Tennessee (for nineteen years now). I am an elementary school teacher. The students I teach are from a low income area. Many of them have never been outside the city. I decided to teach my science and social studies objective by using a unit on Guam. I call it Guam Time. My second grade students look forward to it each day. I have developed the unit over the past two years. I have included many comparing and contrasting activities regarding Guam and Tennessee. I have searched the web and bookstores for information about Guam. I did purchase a couple of books and some souvenirs when I was there. I have also decorated my reading center with a mural of Tarague Beach and a beautiful large fan hand painted in Guam.

I have looked for recipes also, and have cooked several dishes to share with my students. Unfortunately, I did not do a very good job with the cornstarch cookies and the chocolate rice! The latiya cake I made was good. So, I repeated it the second year. I can't wait to try some of yours. I appreciate the precise measurements very much! In May each year, we have a Guam Time celebration for the parents. We make scrapbooks of everything we have learned. We do a power point presentation telling the parents all about Guam and showing them photos. Now you can understand how excited I was to find an actual cookbook. If you are ever in the Johnson City area, let me know. I would love to have you come and talk to my class.

Thanks so much! Brenda Brittain, Johnson City, Tennessee

"GUAM IS GOOD"

Typhoon Greetings!

What amazing technology we live in! My brother, Duncan, sent me your info. Boy, was I delighted! I have so many fond memories of Guam, M.I. (Marianas Island)! Believe it or not, I am still to this day, almost fifty years later, relating my Guam stories to whomever will bend an ear. I, indeed, had a most charmed childhood.

We were a naval military family. In between two tours of duty in Hawaii, we were sent to Guam for eighteen months in 1960. I had my eighth birthday on Guam. I was taught by some of the best teachers there! We went to Piti School, speaking of which, do you have in your cookbook (or can you get) the recipe for the Piti School outrageous tuna-fish sandwich circa 1960? It was a mere 15¢ in those days. I have been trying to duplicate this for about a million years, but somehow cannot come up with it so far. I believe that is the last time I ate white bread! It was super creamy.

The milk they gave us. Yikes! I cannot begin to describe the taste of that stuff. I have yet to come close to anything that smells or tastes like it since! It was all frozen. I think it came from outer space. I heard that the grass the cows fed upon was inferior. Where this milk came from I have no clue, but boy did it taste terrible, way worse than any powdered milk.

Our biggest remembrance of Guam was the sign at the Agaña airport "GUAM IS GOOD".....not to be outdone by my memories of Gabgab Beach. My dad would have parties for the sailors on his destroyer. They would all be down there listening to country music and drinking copious amounts of brew. Back then, there wasn't much on Guam (we called it "the Rock"), except boys riding on caribous down the roads, war dog cemeteries, and jungles galore.

When we first arrived, my four brothers and I took a hike into the jungle. One of them mentioned snakes. I found myself alone when they all tore off at the thought of snakes. We found an abandoned Japanese war plane, old toothbrushes, femurs, skulls, and Japanese yen. When we took the bones home and exclaimed in delight our precious find to our southern grandmother, she implored us to take the bones back to their resting place, because they belonged to somebody's Asian mama!

Most of my little friends were Guamanian. I remember one in particular, Julia Tahaji *(correctly spelled Tajalle)*. She really almost looked Peruvian. The little girls were so poor back then and would come to school in tatters. We had huge jack tournaments at school. I remember there was a large head lice problem. I also remember my black teacher was sent back to the U.S. because of the segregation problems. Times were tough, but we didn't realize any of this until years later. My fondest memory of Piti School was when I caught my brother, Harry, smoking at age twelve. He begged me not to squeal to our mother. Of course, I couldn't wait to get home and tell. He has since passed away last summer. I smile with the thought of that memory. His claim to fame was that he sat behind Bette Midler in Russian class at Radford High School in Hawaii in 1962. They were real chummy. She signed his yearbook in many places.

Let's not forget the dreaded shrews! It's said that grandmother opened up the oven door one night. She was greeted by peering beady little eyes, whereupon, she howled with wild abandon.

There was an abandoned airstrip close by to where we lived. My friend's dad took us there and drove down the airway over 100 miles an hour. It was quite a thrill for a kid.

I do have to tell you, I really dug the typhoons! We would go out in the middle of them, hang from a pole, and let the wind soar our little bodies through the air. What fun! Our house was solid cement (yes, we had the heaters in the closets for the mildew). We would roller skate on the roof of the house. All the windows were louvered.

Guam is steeped with history. I am so thrilled that you are bringing it back on the map. Paula, it has been such a long time since these memories, as I am now fifty-five. I will never forget my memories of Guam. They were a gigantic part of my life. Kudos to you for remembering Guam. I am now employed as a line cook in New Orleans. Yes, Katrina was devastating. I lost all my pictures of Guam, as well as the last 40 years of my life. I shall purchase your cookbook ASAP. Thanks so much!!

Jenny Fawcett, New Orleans, LA

Memories of a Sailor and a Civilian

The following is my interview with Dr. David Marn, D.Ch. stationed on Guam in 1977, only to return in 2005 working for the National Weather Service.

I arrived in Guam in July 1977, serving under the navy and married at the time. I remember just getting off the plane from Hawaii to Guam. As soon as they opened the door of the plane, that humidity in July was just crushing. I lived in the Midwest. It was a shock for both my wife and I. It was such a difference from anything I've ever experienced, that tropical, moist air.

I really liked Guam, because I already liked to travel. It was a little far away, but it was still interesting. It was more a cultural shock than anything, because I grew up in the Midwest. I was nineteen or twenty years old at the time. Seeing the villages and tropical plants were a shock.

I worked at the communication station. We dealt with things that I can't really say. It was at Finegayan, but I lived at the Naval Air Station in married housing. Before we got base housing, I had to live in Dededo for a few months. This was before it really got rough. Dededo was starting to get a reputation back then, about being a little rougher than most.

I used to work the midnight shift with a lot of marines. My job required quite a bit of teletyping. One night, all of a sudden, I am feeling my chair just shake. I'm going, "what in the world." I look back, and didn't see any marines, 'cause sometimes they like to joke around. I wonder to myself how they could move away that fast. I figured I was just imagining something. My chair started shaking again. So, I turned around real fast. Nobody was there. I asked the group who was messing with my chair. Someone said, "Hey, you know that's not us. You just felt an earthquake!" That was my first earthquake – a small one, but coming from the Midwest, we didn't have those.

I didn't venture out much other than driving down Marine drive from base to base. When I wasn't working, we'd go to the beach, do some snorkeling, and ride our bikes.

Another thing that was different – even though I have always had an interest in weather and went to school for weather – was the typhoons. Guam was like a target for typhoons.

The military housing, at that time, had just those louvered windows. When it stormed or had heavy down-pours, we got so much rain through the windows, that it would flood inside our house. We had to put all our furniture or anything expensive up on cinder blocks to keep it from getting wet.

Termites – I remember termites! They would get in easily through the louvers. We had to put a bucket of water at the entry ways. When they flew over it, they would fall into the bucket. I used to end up with buckets of termites coming through at certain times of the year.

My second time on Guam, I didn't even see one termite. I don't know what happened, but that was quite a change for me – not seeing termites during termite season.

Geckos – I used to have, I guess, a family of geckos living in my navy house. I just remember using a sponge to do the dishes. The geckos used to sit there and lick the water out of the sponge.

My first time to Guam, it was during the cold war. Doing the job I did, let's just say, I knew when foreign government's vessels were approaching us. So, I knew where to look. You could see them on the coast if you knew where they were. I was able to see them out at Tumon Bay using binoculars.

It has changed a lot. At Finegayan, they have the big elephant cage. I went back my second time and looked for it. It's a huge array of antennae. The antennae went around this building and probably 70-100 feet tall. Our building was inside that array. You have to drive way back there. Now, they have satellite dishes, but the elephant cage is still there.

My second trip to Guam – I didn't particularly want to go back to Guam, but it was the only job opening I could get in the National Weather Service. The office was located in Barrigada at the old Naval Air Station. I remember I used to ride my bike around there. I saw how bad it had gotten. My house that I used to live in – it looked like a bomb hit the thing. That whole area – what could have happened because it was only 25 years ago?

When I arrived on this second trip, a tropical storm was ready to hit the island. I was staying at a hotel across the street from Naval Air Station – close to where I worked. I happened to be looking at the satellite picture. I thought, "You're kidding me, there's a storm." Before I even started to work, I could see this forming on a little satellite cable feed. "Oh my goodness, what have I done?" I thought to myself.

There were a lot more people this time. Chuukese, Chinese, Koreans – it seemed like they were taking over.

The most obvious thing to me was the change in Tumon Bay and all the hotels.

NCS Beach – My first time to Guam I got rescued with a friend by the Coast Guards at NCS Beach (around the time the movie Jaws had come out). When I was there the second time, I didn't even realize it was the same beach – that's how much it had changed.

Tarague – Although Tarague Beach is still beautiful, it was much more beautiful my first time around.

For my second tour, I lived in the Talofofo area – right behind Jeff's Pirate's Cove. I used to jog back in that area and see lots of boonie dogs. I fed them, and they would run with me. For some reason, they didn't run with me this one day….it was 'cause of a wild pig. This boar came out in front of me and ran from me instead of towards me. I also saw a lot more chickens this time.

One of the first things I noticed was how they repaired the roads. They fill the hole with asphalt. They put enough asphalt to cover just over the hole. They never leveled it out. It's like speed bumps on the road, particularly at the area on the east coast. I lived in Talofofo, and I'd come up through Barrigada.

Food – I had red rice and lumpia. I was mostly vegetarian. I did try beetlenut. A local asked me if I wanted to try it. I asked him what it was. I said I had heard of it. It had some kind of hallucinogenic effect. I tried it and nothing happened. I ended up having three of them. My mouth was dry. I'm sure it was red.

David Marn

An *"almost book"* to Paula

O.k. Paula, here it goes. Hope this doesn't turn into a book of my own!

It was a cold morning in November 1986 when my father told me that I needed to enjoy the last fleeting weeks of winter. I asked him why, because we had just started to get into the cold days of the year.

He then told me that we were moving somewhere where the record lowest temperature ever recorded was 76 degrees. I thought my life was over. I have always liked the winter months more than the summer. I thought he was moving us to hell. Then, when he told me where we were going, I really thought it was going to be hell. He said that the navy had given him orders to Guam, and we would be leaving in the middle of December. December? Not only were we going to somewhere hot and very humid, we were going to miss Christmas and New Years with family and friends. Needless to say, I tried everything in the book not to go with my family to Guam. My dad had a way of looking at things, no matter how bad, in a good light. He told me, "Jake, you need to settle down and enjoy this experience. You will be going somewhere most people will never get to go and only read about in books." Of course, he also said this when we were almost done with our time in Guam, and we were going straight to Japan! That was a total of six years, combined, that we lived outside the Continental U.S. and away from family. But, that's a story for another day.

A week or so later, a moving company came to our house in California. They packed up all our things for the long trip to Guam. I have to admit that once the house was empty, I started to get excited about the move. The internet wasn't even thought of (at least not for use by everyone). Personal computers in the home were a very new concept during that time. So, I had been doing a lot of research at the school library trying to find out anything and everything about this new land I was going to. I had noticed that the waters surrounding Guam looked very clear and inviting, and had talked my dad into (maybe) taking some scuba classes so we could enjoy the island to the fullest. When we left California, it was initially just my dad and I. My mom and brother stayed to complete the sale of our house.

When we landed in Guam, the first thing I remember was getting off the plane, and getting "punched" by the humidity. BAM! Instant sweat and a desire for an immediate shower was all I felt. It was a real drastic change in climate for me. I had never lived in a place were humidity could even be felt, so thick you could reach out and cut it with a knife. The next big change was the time difference. The first night on Guam, my dad and I tried to go to bed when it got dark. It wasn't dark where we just came from. When I woke up later, it felt like I had just taken a nap. I laid there in bed at the hotel room thinking, "So what am I going to do now? I can't get up and do anything because it's the middle of the night. I really don't want to wake up dad." Then, I heard my father call my name very faintly from the other room. He was awake too! He said, "Jake, are you awake?" I said, "Yes," and told him I was very hungry. He said, "Well, it is after midnight (so technically it is morning). Let's go get some breakfast." So, it is like two or three in the morning, in a new place, and we hop into the rental car for our first adventure of many on Guam….going to find something to eat. I don't remember where it was that we ate that morning, but I do remember wanting it to get light so I could explore this wonderful, new place we had just gotten to.

That's the introduction to my life on Guam. If I did a play by play, I could write a book of my own….

I did get my dad to cave in and pay for scuba lessons (he even took the classes with me) which was a major accomplishment since my dad hated to spend money. We spent the next few years going on many dives, exploring the wonderful and beautiful underwater world that exists just below the surface. I have been diving constantly since then. I have never been to anywhere where the water was that clear or that warm. I loved the fact that you didn't need to fuss with a wet suit to enjoy a dive. I could just strap on the tank and jump into the water!

My dad made it a common practice that whereever we lived, he would get together with a local person and learn one new word every day. He always wanted to learn the language of where we were. He said that this was a way to respect the people of the area where you lived…after all, you were in THEIR home, not the other way around. My dad had a very good memory. He could always remember every word taught to him. The Chamorro friends he made while we lived on Guam would always tell him "thank-you" for respecting them enough to try to learn the language. After the few years we lived there, he got quite fluent in the language. I too tried to do this in Guam, as well as when we moved to Japan, but my memory and word ennunciation was no match for my father's.

My dad was a very friendly guy. He got along with almost everyone. Our Guam experience was no exception. We were invited to many fiestas while we were on Guam. So many, that it seemed like we were going to one, two, or three every month. I don't remember my mom cooking very much while we were there, which is strange. She always had something cooking before we moved, and since we left. We were always given TONS of leftovers to take home with us when we left a fiesta. I really do miss the food of Guam, and have tried to replicate it myself (see cookbook "A Taste of Guam" for some excellent recipes). However, you can never make the food taste the same as someone that has been cooking if for as long as the Chamorro people have. I have even had authentic ingredients (lemon powder, boonie peppers, etc.) sent to me from Guam. It's still not the same….not even close. By the way, can someone send me some beetle-nuts please!

Living on Guam was wonderful, but, occasionally, even the thrill of living on an island was crushed. We lived through many typhoons while we lived there. The worst one was Typhoon Roy. It destroyed most of the island. Power was off for weeks. Almost all of the landmarks we had come to love and enjoy were gone! Farmer's Market – gone! Two Lover's Point statue – gone! Lots and lots of our Chamorro friends' homes – gone!! We were fortunate enough to live in base housing, which was reinforced concrete block, as much of the military structures were. Still, with no electricity it was like living a virtual "Gilligan's Island."

I loved living on Guam so much that I have been back once since then. I was on my own. I am saving up to go again in the near future. Just the plane ticket alone will kill your wallet! I still, even to this day, think of Guam on a daily basis. I have put the "Guam Seal" sticker on every truck I have owned since I left Guam. I will say, I do get quite a stare or sometimes even a chuckle out of a Chamorro that will pass me on the freeway or in a parking lot. I suspect that when they see the Seal, they are expecting to see a fellow Chamorro….not a big, white "Hoalie!" I love Guam, and would like some day to be able to return, and never leave. With the limit to the jobs one can find on the "Tiny Island," I will probably have to wait till I retire to move there for good.

Well Paula, thank you for letting me share my experiences of Guam with you.

Thanks again and Hafa Adai!
Jake Milson

An interview with Kathy Duenas Sulovski

I remember my grandmother would make boñelos dågo. We would eat it every New Year's. We would also sell boñelos dågo and pickle papaya around the neighborhood and at bingo.

My cousins and I would all meet at my grandmother's house. I remember playing cockfight with the flame tree. That was our game with my cousins. We used to go around the island every weekend. Guam was very beautiful. As we grew older, everyone kind of scattered.

I went to St. Anthony's with the nuns. There were three of us, myself and my two siblings. I miss the parties.

I represented J.F.K. High School as Ms. J.F.K. in the Guam Liberation queen's court. That is how I met Kevin, my husband, as he was my escort at the Asan Park celebration in 1976.

Kathy Duenas Sulovski
Originally from Tamuning, Guam
Currently residing in Newton Grove, NC

An interview with Edward Blas Cruz

I played baseball a lot on Guam. There were lots of dances and dj's: Battle of the Bands, the pony, cha-cha, rhomba, jitterbug, båtsu. I remember Hong Kong Gardens. It was a hall for weddings, graduations, and proms in 1967. It was situated over the water in Tamuning. It was a gathering place for teenagers during the days of the Beetles, rock 'n roll, the BG's, Simon & Garfunkel.

I played baseball with Eddie Aguon, Ted Taijeron, Tony Aguon, and Tony Mariano.

I love my parents. They lived a long time. They taught me so many things. Respect my elders no matter what. Help anybody that needs help. Even if you have no money, you can help with your hands and your knowledge. If I owed money, to pay it back in kind, and more, such that they know how grateful I was for their help.

I never knew how to cook. However, because I saw the importance of what my mom and dad showed in entertaining others, I was able to cook the food by having eaten the food they cooked for us.

During Christmas time, we went caroling throughout the village. I was in the Young American Choir in Barrigada. We were invited to Anderson Air Force Base and the Naval Officers Club. They fed us good after our performances.

I was in the apprenticeship program at the Piti Powerplant with a few of my high school friends, like Henry Pangelinan and Tony Mariano. We studied to be journeymen in our field – power plant control men. During the Vietnam War, there were so many apprenticeship programs: for carpenters, electricians, diesel operators. I finished my program in three and a half years and became a journeyman.

My wife had to go to training in the mainland. At that time, she also applied for a position and accepted the offer. The job gave her an increase in pay and paid for moving expenses. I decided to take a vacation from my job. I headed out to the states with my five kids. This is how we moved off-island. When we came to the states, they were rationing gasoline. We sat in line waiting to get gas. It was 1978.

My father was one of the Japanese slaves during WWII. His name is Jesus Guerrero Cruz. He was born on March 1st, 1912. He was a former carpenter and worked a little bit for the Government of Guam. He devoted his life to full-time farming in Barrigada. He grew corn, watermelon, honeydew, cantaloupe, cucumber, green beans, lima beans, bananas, papayas, sweet potatoes, tsunin-Honolulu, and tsuni-agaga. He also had pipino – the white, sweet version of honeydew.

I was one of fourteen kids. Three died during the war. One of those three died in my father's arms in the march from Manenggon to Yigo.

For breakfast, I remember drinking Carnation milk, eating scrambled eggs, pancakes, and Quaker Oatmeal Cereal. My mom made lots of kåddon kåtne, kåddon månnok, chalakiles, estufao, cornsoup, soup Tan Candelaria (beef-vegetable soup), bistek, chicken kelaguen, fried chicken, and bbq. In the late 50's, early 60's, I remember my sisters would make tamales mendioka.

I remember my dad would collect tuba and make binaklen tuba (vinegar), too. As a young adult, my dad would hide from the feds because he was also making moonshine!

Edward Blas Cruz
Originally from Radio Barrigada
Currently in Glen Burnie, Maryland

A Tale of Two Sisters

LuAnn Cruz Ramirez and Debra Easley

I was so fortunate that two of my mom's sisters, Auntie Lulu and Auntie Debbie, took time to come visit me this year. The following is a transcription of their trip down memory lane. It was priceless to get a glimpse of what their lives were like.

Lu: I was sleeping when Sharlene came to me and said Agnes slapped her. So, I went over to Agnes's house to see why she slapped Sharlene. All Maman Biha *(translated as grandmother)* saw was me hitting Agnes. We were fighting. Maman Biha grabbed the cow tail whip and chased me and Debbie.

Deb: *We ran back to our house and Auntie Lu hid in the kiss-a-me. I ran between the beds. Maman Biha saw me and she whipped me. I didn't even do anything. I saw Auntie Lu. She was peeking out and laughing.*

Lu: I was going to go under the bed, but Cheryl told me they would find me. She told me to go up to the kiss-a-me. I was scared because I didn't know what was up there. But, I went anyways because I didn't want to get caught. I could see Maman Biha in the room, just looking, fuming. I could see how angry she was because she couldn't find me. She went home. My dad always stopped by his mom's house before he came home. Boy, she let him have it. He was so mad at her he punched the front door and put a hole in it.

Lu: I was scared as heck for my dad to come home. I was already crying before he got home. I cried every time one of my brothers asked me what happened. When dad finally got home, I told him what happened. He said, "Good for you!" Dad was so mad that he finally decided to move us out of Canada, Barrigada.

Lu: We moved to Agana Heights. It was so funny because we only had four bedrooms. One was for our parents, the other for your mom, one for Uncle Jesse, and the middle room was shared by the other six of us. It was like the military – you know the cots and everything. We had two bunk beds and two single beds. All of us didn't sleep at the same time.

Lu: My brothers hung out late. We never ate dinner together. It was like a wave: the young ones first, then the older ones, then the oldest ones that came in at 2 a.m. and tried to scarf up what was left in the kitchen.

Lu: Everywhere Auntie Cheryl went, she had to drag me along. She didn't like it because I was always telling on her.

Lu: Then, I started to know everyone. I became a tomboy. We started playing skateboard, studicks. Studicks was a game we made up. You had two posts and those were your bases. There was five in one team, five in the other. If you got out of your base, that means whoever gets out second, can tag you. You can go back and tag your base then try to tag that person back. We ran literally all the way to Sinajana. We didn't have any borders.

Deb: *We would climb trees. It was a made-up game. This was before Typhoon Pamela. We watched Typhoon Pamela. We watched everything fly from the chickens, to the cows, to the pigs.*

Lu: The house got sort-of flooded, but my mom already put everything off of the floor. We were just sliding in the house. We lived near the Sinajana post office.

Deb: *When Typhoon Pamela hit, we lost power for a long time. They built an outside kitchen and we had to cook outside. We learned how to make fire on our own.*

Lu: We brought our games from Canada to Agana Heights and Sinajana. Every game there was, we played it on that street in front of our house: softball, basketball, skate board.

Lu: We had a neighbor, his name was Jo Brown. He would go out there and play games by himself. He would literally be out there when nobody was outside. He would play basketball with no basketball. He was simulating a game.

Deb: We would sit on the sidewalk and watch him.

Lu: Or, we would peek out the window. I think he envisioned there was a team out there. He would high-five everyone, talk to the bench, etc.

Deb: We all clapped when he said "Yeah."

Lu: He'll yell at the referee. He'll shoot the ball and say "Yeah." He was the light of our day.

Deb: Back in the day, the candies were five cents. We used to buy that lipstick candy and put lipstick on us. Then they had that bottle cap candy that's like wax. We used to go to Tan Mary's store to play the pinball machine.

Lu: I miss that game because you can win money out of it. It was like a mini casino. That is probably how we first started to become gamblers. Everybody was addicted to that machine. She only had one pinball machine too! Jeffrey was a pro at it.

Deb: We even played båto (a game of tossing quarters into a hole dug in the ground). The boys had their own stuff. They could take apart a motorcycle in one day and fix it back the same day.

Lu: We fixed everything. If our bikes were broken, the boys were quick to fix it because you literally had to make your own toys. If you broke it, you had to fix it.

Lu: But boy, don't you come home if you had an injury because Grandpa Cruz, oh, he's like Doctor Cruz.

Deb: Remember the mountain we called Charlie Corn's Grave?

Lu: Legend says that Charlie Corn was buried on that mountain so that's why we call it Charlie Corn's Grave. That mountain was right behind our house. Well, it was really a big hill, but from where we were at, it looked like a mountain. On the top, it had what looked like a little house. *(Google "Charlie Corn's Grave" to find some interesting information!).*

Deb: Uncle Bill tried to bike that mountain. He went down first and the motorcycle came right behind him. He broke his arm!

Lu: Whenever my dad had to leave, Grandma Cruz would tell the boys to go get that girl (me) because I was out so late. She couldn't just send one of the boys, she had to send two. If she sent one, he couldn't catch me because I would run around the cars forever. They would get tired and pissed off. So, she always sent two of them. Of course, I would give up 'cause there was no way I could run from them.

Deb: In 1978 we moved from Agana Heights to GHURA 503, now Fern Terrace. There was no grass, just gravel. We had to spread the gravel out ourselves and put Chinese grass in too. . When Auntie Cheryl and Uncle Daso got married, it was still red dirt all over the place.

Lu: Your dad just started painting grandma's house with the diamonds.

Deb: Yeah, the Charlie Brown style.

Lu: Dad thought he would straighten all of us up by putting us in the 4-H Club.

Lu: One day, Deb and I went riding our bikes. The bike had no working brakes so she went straight through the jungle!

Deb: One car was coming this way, the other car that way, and there was no where else to turn, so I avoided both cars and went into the boonie area. I didn't have any type of brakes! I walked out and looked at both cars. They asked if I was ok. I said, "I'm ok." I looked at my knees and they were bleeding. They were all laughing at me!

Lu: She must have gone in fifty feet. I'm at the side laughing.

Deb: They were all laughing. That was my most embarrassing moment. I didn't even want to get on the bike again.

Lu: Remember when Bill tried to teach us how to flip from the roof of the house? Well, Debbie flipped and she didn't hold on to the bike. I told her not that kind of flip!

Deb: I went down hard!

Lu: I remember him teaching us how to jump into the sand box. He said he didn't put no nails or glass, "It's just a box of sand!" This was a Bruce Lee year. Bill was making chuck-sticks and learning how to jump. He said we could learn how to fight, fly, and everything if we would just learn how to jump.

Lu: We were dumb enough and young enough to try it. He said "Get on top of the car and jump into the sand box."

Lu: Bill got so mad at Debbie one day he did a Bruce Lee move and poked his finger right into her eye.

Deb: Yeah, it bled and grandpa got him good too.

Deb: When we got hurt we didn't want them to see it! When they found out, Maman Biha would call us into the house and they would hold us down. They would squeeze that puss out.

Lu: They take the pupulu, the donni, the salt. They stuck that thing in the wound. We'd scream, but we couldn't kick. So, we learned that when we got hurt, we try not to tell anyone because we didn't want to go through that pain.

Deb: They sit on us, hold us down, and squeeze the hell out of that puss. They boil water, they squeeze the hot pepper, they chew the pupulu, and put it all on. Oh lord, they tortured us!

LuAnn Ramirez and Debra Easley

Tidbits

I remember…

Tapioca – *Perlene Lujan, North Carolina*

The beach – *Tammy Rivera, South Carolina*

Family: where I learned the definition of respect. Chotde, Townhouse, PayLess – *Tiara Johnson*

Fiestas, the beach, swimming with underwear – *Kimberly Blas*

The best place in the world to be….growing up in the ranch – *Jeannine Diaz-Hatig*

Hey boy, you got lemai over there…..baseball games, christenings, bibas…we used to drink in the car with no seat belts…they used to make us kids drive – *Jarette Leon Guerrero*

We went looking for a swimsuit to swim in the ocean – *Janessa Pangelinan, South Carolina*

The beach, fiestas, the parade, family, Matåpang Beach, Pleasure Island – *Keilani Blas*

The beach, fiestas, the sun, dukduk (tiny hermit crabs), ayuyu (land crabs), Gef Pågu (island cultural center) – *Kayla Blas*

Chicken, roosters, baby chicks – *Carson E. Lujan Quinene, North Carolina……my boy!*

Bear rock, camel rock – *Manuel Blas*

Crying so bad because I was leaving my family and my wife to a world I didn't know, not knowing what to expect. Typhoon Karen – took away my mom's house. The 2x12 boards fell down. I was one of the boys that huddled around her when the roof flew away. I was knocked unconscious by the same board that broke her collar bone. I had head and eye pain daily. There was a soft spot on my head for six months. *Uncle Jerry Quenga, South Carolina*

I remember Typhoon Omar. We were sitting around grandma's living room. I remember the candles, playing war, solitary, and all the card games that kept us busy. *Tiara*

I remember the beaches on Guam and the Chamorro food that the people make. Guam is a very nice island to live on.
Johanna Cabe, Canada, Barrigada

What I remember most about Guam are the beaches at night. I'd go for a walk and I could hear the water hitting the sand. I remember going fishing with my dad at five or six in the morning. I miss drinking the juice from the coconuts and eating the middle part from the tree. I remember spending the weekends at the ranch, going through the typhoons...LOL. I miss the power outages, going to hula classes. I miss my friends and my family! I miss Guam!
Jenell Taijeron
Cheyenne, Wyoming

I remember a lot about Guam, most especially my family, my friends, the beaches, and the culture.
Cheryl Lynn C. Blend
Houston/Humble, Texas

I remember the good weather, the climate, bbq parties at the beach or ranch, visiting on Thanksgiving, Christmas, etc. I remember at grandma's house we were having a pretty bad typhoon...but we were all together with my mom and siblings. Kind of scary, though fun afterwards. Guam is good!
Joshua Cabe
Y-PAOPAO Estates, Dededo, Guam

I remember all the parties on the weekends and getting together with all the cousins. We had a great time. I remember growing up in Dededo and attending Santa Barbara Catholic School. I remember what the air would smell like after it rained. I remember an island with a proud heritage and culture. Most importantly, I remember my family. *Ryan Flauta, Florida*

I miss the family gatherings, the big parties, and basically, feeling the warm sun on my skin. I enjoyed my life on Guam when I lived there for about nine years! It's where I am from and where I represent!
Jonathan Manglona

Hi Paula! I know your brothers! What I remember about Guam are the beaches, my family, my friends, and the food. I remember the parties and the long nights out with friends.
Yvonne Cruz

Memoirs of

Mrs. Dolores Mesa Jones

Wife to Mack Jones of
Jones & Guerrrero

DOLORES JONES
Interviewed on August 18, 2007

My dad was a poor farmer's son. My grandpa sent my dad to the Phillippines. He rode a clipper from Sumay to Manila to go to college. My dad neglected his studies because his teacher was my mother, Maria. They got married in the Phillippines. My mom's side was rich and disowned her for marrying a poor Guamanian farmer's boy.

When my dad and mom went back to Guam, he was disowned because he married a Filipina. Back then, you were supposed to marry the girl next door.

Both of my parents taught in the schools. The new family moved a lot. My mom was transferred as a teacher and as a principal. We were in Merizo in 1938 for two years. My family lived in the Merizo school. We would go to the bantalån – pier – and we would eat there. There was no kitchen in the school. Sometimes, we would stand on the fish box and dive in. The box would flip over and all the fish came out. We would run home. The whole village went to the bantalån to swim. Going to school in Merizo, our PE was to swim everyday.

My mom was very educated. She sent dad to school in the Phillippines to be a dentist. This happened before the war. Every summer when father came home, mother got pregnant. There were eight kids in all. My mom supported eight kids on her own while father was in dental school. Before the war, mom had sent two of her boys to the Phillippines to go to school. She felt boys needed more education. She also sent one girl.

My mom had five maids on Guam. Her friends sent their daughters to be her maids. My family sold popsicles, sandwiches, and homemade soup at Lerry School in Agaña. My family had our laundry sent out to be washed in the river. They would lay the clothes out on the grass. The clothes were returned nice and ironed.

Mother made soap and bartered it for papaya and breadfruit. She couldn't really sell the soap 'cause no one had the money to buy it. The big pot that she made the soap in was cooking all the time. Sometimes, she had to go to Cocos Island to get the big log to make the ashes.

I never got a whipping from my dad. My mom was the one to whip me. When mom would try to get me, I would run between my dad's legs and say, "Dad, mom is going to get me." He would say, "Suha, suha Maria. Don't you touch my girl." He was a great father.

My mom gave me good advice, she said, "Daughter, sex is wonderful, but you gotta do it with your husband."

Church
We had to go to mass every morning, all of us, at 5 a.m. I had to go to school, then catechism after school. I didn't know how to speak Chamorro as a kid because mom was Filipina. She didn't want us to speak Chamorro, only English. At catechism one day, the teacher told me to get up and say the Lord's Prayer in Chamorro. I said, "I don't know." I stayed in the same grade every year for catechism. Every year I got bigger and bigger. My classmates got smaller and smaller. I never received Holy Communion till I was fourteen years old. Finally, the priest made an exception for me to pass and receive communion. That day, I was the last one in line. They thought I was the teacher. When my mom died, I learned how to speak Chamorro.

When I was already married, every time we went to church, they always had empanada for sale as a fundraising.

Food
We ate fish everyday. We raised our own chicken. When we slaughtered the pig, we shared with the neighbors. We made fritåda. We had a ranch in Dededo. Dad had twenty hectares and hunted wild boars. We caught a lot of ayuyu and pånglao. There was titiyas, breadfruit, taro, tapioca, åhu, and red rice before the war.

I was about six years old when I had to go door to door to sell poto before I went to school. My mom told me, "Don't come back till you sell all of it!" Sometimes, when I had one or two left, I would eat it.

In the old days, they would bbq lemai. We would eat it with mantakiyan babui (pig fat). My father always had a trap for pig and binådu (deer). We always had binådu in our deep freeze. That helped with our groceries. We didn't have to buy meat. My father loved kelaguen binådu, dried, wild pig, and bbq.

A young girl's life on Guam

My father told me, "Don't ever go to your boyfriend's house. Let him come here!" I don't like to drink or smoke. My dad told me I could do it, but do it in front of him. People on Guam were very strict. All my girlfriends cannot go out on dates. They cannot even look out the window. The Mesas were the wild ones in Sinajana. We go out and climb the breadfruit trees.

One of my best friends said to me, "Linga, fana'an adai mapotge yu *(I think I am pregnant)*." Dolores replied, "Håfa un chogue *(what did you do)*." Her girlfriend said, "Ha chiko yu *(he kissed me)*." *(At this point, Dolores and I were both laughing quite intensely!)* My friend's moms were so strict with their daughters. I had to pretend we were going to my house. They knew and respected my mom. So, they trusted me to take their daughters out. I always warned my friends to keep their legs closed because I was responsible for them! That is the only thing I don't understand about the Chamorro culture. How could you find a boyfriend? When you get caught with a boy they want you to marry him even if you don't like the boy. They think you are pregnant.

Before the war, there was no road from Umatac to Agat. So, Umatac people had to go through Merizo then Inarajan. We used to fight with people from Umatac. We wouldn't let them pass. The same thing happened with Inarajan. We'll fight with them. They wouldn't let us pass. We have to wait till dark to pass because there's only one way.

The people in Agaña thought they were it. They used to tease people from Merizo that all they ate was pånglao and gumson *(crab and octopus)*. They didn't know how good it was! In the old days it was fun. When the atulai *(fish)* comes in, everybody goes out and everybody gets a share. They divided the catch. But, then we got modern. The fishermen used the boats and nets. They would sell the atulai. One day, the atulai didn't come in. We said, "See, lalå'lu si Yu'us sa they didn't share"…..same with the mañåhåk *(fish also)*. During the Japanese time, they used hand grenades. They threw the grenades in and they're (the fish) dead. You have to jump in. You come up with some in your hands and some in your mouth. The galaide *(boat)* was there so you could throw it in.

As far as canned goods, we mainly used Carnation milk. One day, my mom sent me to ask for ten cents from my grandfather for Carnation milk. He sent me home with rice. My mom was so mad, she threw it out!

My mom used the big flour sacks for panties. The rubber from the tire was used for the elastic. Panties and pillows were numbered for each of us five girls.

Japanese Invasion
In Agaña, when the bombing started, everybody was at church. Father Scott told everyone to go and hide at your ranch. So, we went home and took what we could. We went to Tumon. Mom had sent all the men away in the house. Mom saw soldiers and called them over. She thought they were Americans, but they were Japanese.

Japanese Occupation
Everyone who was six years old to seventy years old had to work in the field. I lived in Merizo at the time. I had to plant rice and green vegetables! We had to feed the Japanese soldiers. Their ships were not coming in any more, so they had no food. It was forced labor. You had to be working or be at a Japanese school. The Japanese would count the number of banana bunches, chicken, and pigs we had.

One day a Japanese school teacher came to our house and wanted my mother's sewing machine. My mother said no. He slapped my mom, so she got the scissors. My mom told me to call Taichu, a Japanese soldier. I told him mom needed help. Taichu brought the school teacher out into the yard and slapped him. My mother always gave Taichu cigarettes and eggs. My mother would not bow to the Japanese teacher.

I heard some Chamorros hid in the caves during the war. My girlfriend said she had never saw Japanese before.

Weeks before American liberation

I got bitten by a Japanese dog so I did not work for one day. When I went back to work, I got hit, I got slapped, and I got tied to a coconut tree. I thought I was going to get killed. The soldier untied me. By the time I was home, my mother was already gone. They took thirty people from Merizo.

SASALAGUAN – Mom was taken to a fox hole. They were told to hide from bombs. The Japanese threw hand grenades into the fox hole. When the Japanese went back inside, they were told to kill anything that moved. One lady, Lisa, said that my mom asked to spare her life because she had kids.

It started to rain really hard. I think the Lord was on our side because the Japanese left the entrance of the fox hole. Afterwards, some of those people came out of the fox hole. They went back to Merizo. Some of them got a canoe because they saw a ship and were trying to signal them.

After the U.S. recaptured the island

They set up camps on the island. A lot of people died from dysentery and diarrhea. An Agat commander took over the orphans. We stayed in the tombs. Nothing was covering us on top, rain or shine. The Marines fed us. We stayed with various families till we could get to my relatives. After about a month, we were reunited with my family. We stayed near the Ilig River. Every time it rained, the river overflowed. We moved to Talofofo for a while where my uncle built a nice, big "A" frame. We had to get up every morning and get in line for water.

In 1945, my father came back from the Phillippines and took us to Sinajana. We stayed there for ten years.

Mack & Dolores

When I started going out with this haolie my father said, "Linga, why are you going to go out with this white man because you are black?" Later, I said, "I think I am going to marry him dad." Dad said, "He eats cabbage, potatoes, and steak. We eat rice and fish." I said, "Dad, I could learn to like those things." He said, "Your marriage will never last. He is white and you are black. When he goes home he will not even want to introduce you to his family."

My dad passed away a long time ago.

Mack and I have been married fifty-five years. *(She looks to the heavens and says)* "See dad, I'm still married to the same man *(she is laughing and smiling as she speaks)*." I could tell she loved her dad and respected him.

"Dad, I need a medal, a gold one, a gold medal." Not too many Chamorro girls married a haoli. I never distinguished color. Intermarriage is a no-no in Guam.

My husband is a Baptist, but I told my husband before we got married, "You have to become a Catholic." He took catechism, was baptized, and then we got married.

We were married on Guam in 1952. Our first house was a quonset hut. Then the company upgraded the housing. We moved to where the new houses were built or available. We kept moving like the umang, the hermit crab. Initially, we had ½ of a quanset hut. Three months later, we got a full hut. Then, at lower J&G a ½ prefab was available, then a full prefab. After Typhoon Karen, we moved to Jonestown where they built a house. It was the second and third increment. Once J & G started to build concrete houses, we had to buy the house.

Dolores Mesa Jones
Garner, NC

Events, Places, Traditions

Guam Liberation Day Celebrations

Guam was invaded and occupied for over 2.5 years by the Japanese during WWII. We were liberated by the United States on July 21, 1944. We celebrate this turning point every year with many festivities on Guam and throughout the world!

Wherever you may go, where there is a large number of Chamorros, keep an eye out during the summer time. You may be lucky to bump into a Guam Liberation Day fiesta!

Liberation Day Parade – For many years, my family would meet somewhere along Marine Drive, along the parade route in Agaña / Anigua. Some years, we would have a canopy for a cover, other years we would brave the sun and rain with umbrellas. For a few years, my dad made a make shift canopy with his gray tow truck.

While waiting for the parade to start, most attendees were anxious to buy ice-kekee (a heartier version of the "Flavor-ice"). This ice candy on Guam comes in a long, cylindrical, shaped tube about an inch in diameter. The typical flavors and colors are orange, blue, red, yellow etc. The best ones though, were brought in from Saipan. My favorite was the coconut flavored ice-kekee. There was also ice-kekee in some pretty interesting shapes: think big, bulky Christmas ornaments.

Towards the Anigua end of the parade route, there was this little store, ACME. Our favorite venture before the parade began, was to head to ACME and buy some "bubble things." I believe they sell it here in the states: squeeze the goop onto the edge of the tiny straw, blow on the straw and walla, you have a bubble that does not pop as fast as a soap bubble.

Carnival

I looked forward to summer on Guam because I enjoyed the carnival!

The location of the carnival on Guam changed every couple of years: most of the time it was in Agaña, at the Paseo, some years it was at the Yigo Amusement Park. I believe it may have been held at the Town House parking lot, Asan Park, and Ypao Beach too.

The carnival was a tiny, tiny version of a state fair, Chamorro style. This was always a great place to get bbq, can't seem to get enough of it! Then there is this ball game: "Place your bets, place your bets, hands off the counter, and the ball goes rolling and rolling to the lucky color of blue, pay blue, pay blue, pay blue." I was just a kid at the time. At every carnival, I could count on that familiar chant.

One year, I rode this thing called the octopus. It really looked like an octopus: big oval head in the center, eight long arms extending out. Ugh, I was so scared of the ride I cried the entire time. The whole ride turned round and round. The arms moved up and down!

Christenings / Baptismals

Christening parties on Guam are as involved as wedding parties (fandangos). Many families, especially during the 1970's, 1980's, and 1990's, had huge christening parties.

The "largeness" of a party is typically noted by how much food was put out on the tables: the # of rice pots (pots so big men could barely wrap their arms around it); the # of cases of meat / chicken; so many containers of kelaguen or potato salad etc. Also, there is a tendency to compete with how many people attended the party.

The baby's area, a place at the party to see and hold the baby, was elaborately decorated. There are usually several canopies put up, a bar for all sorts of drinks, and several long tables of food. Entertainment may be in the form of any or all of the following: a DJ, a band, and local dancers.

One of the things most children enjoyed at christening parties was the biba. A biba is when the godparents of the baby throw out coins to the waiting crowd of children.

I slightly remember the party my family threw for my youngest brother, Timmy. We lived in GHURA 506 at the time. There were canopies on either side of the house, the back, and one in the front. I was just over seven years old, but I do remember having lots of family there: from immediate family members to my grandmother's sisters, her nieces, and her nephews. Life on Guam was all about family and friends.

As a teenager growing up on Guam, I did not quite understand why parents would throw such parties for babies who would not even remember this event. I now realize it was not just about the baby. It was more about gathering friends and families together to celebrate the new life, to celebrate our Chamorro culture.

Christmas on Guam

I love Christmas on Guam! I am very blessed to have lived on Guam in the 70's, 80's, and 90's. During those decades, most of the island's people were Catholics. If you can imagine a Catholic Christmas in the mainland, magnify it a thousand fold and you would have a slight idea of what Christmas on Guam was like. The entire island was decorated with Christmas lights: the neighborhoods, hotel row, Marine Drive, Town House, Gibsons, Ben Franklin, Guam Power Authority etc.

My favorite tradition during this holiday was the nobena. It is nine days of prayer, song, and food. As a young girl growing up, my parents and my siblings attended the following three nobenas: my mom's, Auntie Kit's, and my Grandma Cruz's nobena. My Grandma Cruz was a techa, a man or a woman who leads the prayer and singing. We would start with the sign of the cross. We would pray in Chamorro, sing 3-4 songs, and end with the sign of the cross. Afterwards, all the young ones would get up and amen those who were older than they were. While everyone was paying respects to the elders, some of the family members would pass out the food for the evening: soup, sandwiches, dessert, bettlenut & pupulu, coffee etc. On the last night of the nobena, we would have a good ole Chamorro bbq, sometimes a grand feast!

A "Cruz" Down Memory Lane

Below is a friend's recollection of landmarks on Guam.

A&W – on East Agaña, across the bay. I'm not sure what is in its place right now. I believe it is a funeral home. They also had putt-putt golf.

Snow White – in Anigua. KFC is now in that location.

Mark's Walgreen then connected with Mark's Department Store – in Anigua next to Snow White / KFC.

Rocco's Pizza – at the intersection of route 10 and the road to UOG. I don't remember what it was before the pizza place. I remember they had pretty good pizza. But for a kid, any pizza is good pizza.

Tony's (or was it Tommy's?) Ice Cream – I think it was in Merizo. I just remember that it was almost exactly half way through our trip around the southern part of the island. Whenever we would do that "road trip," we'd always stop there for burgers and then ice cream.

Julale Shopping Center – did anyone realize this was the first "real" mall on Guam? I remember that when it opened, I thought it was weird to have all the stores in one place. I loved it though, because they had great stores, a coffee shop, and a bank on the first floor. I remember in the 3rd grade, we did a show there during Christmas time.

Agaña Theatre – now the location for Stay Well Insurance. The building to the right of it used to be a medical center. I'm not quite sure what it was called.

Bank of America – it used to be a small building where Bank of Hawaii is today.

Family Shoe Store – used to be where the big Bank of Guam is now. We always got our oxfords and uniforms for San Vicente there.

J & G PayLess – used to be where Bunny Hardware is now. Town House furniture was next to them.

Town House Department Store – used to be where Nissan is now.

Ben Franklin – used to be where Sharp is now before they moved across the street.

Shakey's Pizza – it was where Lonestar Restaurant currently is.

Cruz Wholesale – used to be in Maite. I don't remember what is in its place, but I believe a fire destroyed the building.

Suzuki Motors – used to be where Agaña Beach Hotel is on East Agana Bay.

Allen Sekt – he was a car dealer, but I cannot remember where he was located. He and Chick from Chick's Chrysler were pretty popular. Chicks used to be located at the intersection of Marine Drive and Ypao Beach Road in Tamuning.

Fe Cruz Thornton
Fort Worth, Texas

TITA'S BAKERY

What would we do without Tita's Bakery?

Ben and Mariquita "Tita" Calvo Leon Guerrero.

LOCATION / MAILING ADDRESS
928A Cross Island Road, Santa Rita, Guam 96915

PHONE   671-565-2013   **FAX**   671-565-9565.

EMAIL   titajr@guam.net

I went home in December 1999 for a perfect vacation. I was determined to stop by and visit with Tita. Of course, I did not set up an appointment to see her. Hence, I was only able to take a picture at the front of her bakery.

The History of Tita's Bakery

Tita wanted to provide her daughters with a Catholic school education. This required a second family income.

During her girl's early childhood years, Tita made guyuria for family and friends. They loved it! Tita began to receive many orders! Making guyuria, eventually, became a full time job.

In the beginning, Tita sold guyuria to government offices and the mom & pop stores on island. Tita's bakery, still operating out of her home in Santa Rita, now provides guyuria throughout the entire island of Guam. Additionally, her hard work and determination has enabled her to package Tita's Guyuria such that they may be shipped to countries around the world.

Tita was awarded the 2000 Governor's Magalåhi Lifetime Award. This honor is bestowed upon individuals or organizations that have fostered and nurtured the Chamorro culture. Tita credits her grandfather, Tun Pedro Ada, for her business and work ethics that have helped to make her bakery so successful.

CHODE

Guam's one stop shop for breakfast on the go!
Chode is THE place to buy local specialties like empanåda, pantosta, månha titiyas, yeast doughnuts, poto, and more. Chode has been serving Guam since 1968.

LOCATION / MAILING ADDRESS
125 9th St., Hagåtña, Guam 96910

PHONE 671-477-1524   **FAX** 671-472-6790

Where does the RED in RED RICE come from?

The RED in RED RICE comes from the achote *(annatto)* seed. This picture was taken at a Quinene family home. I remember when my Grandma Cabe had an achote tree in the front of her property. It was fun to pick the seeds out of the pods. We had to pick quite a bit of them as there was only about a teaspoon's worth of achote seeds in each pod. The seeds needed to be soaked in water. After soaking for a few hours, the seeds were rubbed between the palms of the hands to release the color and flavor into the water. This water was then used to make red rice *(neksa agaga)*.

I did not find any other country that used the achote for rice as the Chamorros do to make red rice. Several countries use it to flavor their rice, but use it as an accompanying or minute flavor. For example, in Cuba, only 1/8th of a teaspoon is used to flavor the rice.

Likewise, many places, Guam included, use the achote to flavor or color meats and soups. Furthermore, achote is used as a coloring for cheese, fabric dye, arts & crafts, and body paint.

Personally, I love how the achote transforms white rice: color ranging from bright orange, to a beautiful burnt, red. The flavor is unmistakable. One lazy day, I used the Goya substitute to make red rice. Carson, my son, would not eat it! He said, "Mommy, this is not real red rice. I don't like it." Hmph, can't use Goya anymore and expect him to eat it!

HUSKING A COCONUT

The pick-ax is plunged into the ground. The coconut is pushed over the sharp, narrow end of the pick-ax until the inner nut is reached. Then, the husk is torn against the ax and pulled away.

This process is continued until all the husk is removed from the nut. The coconut in this picture is actually a young coconut or månha.

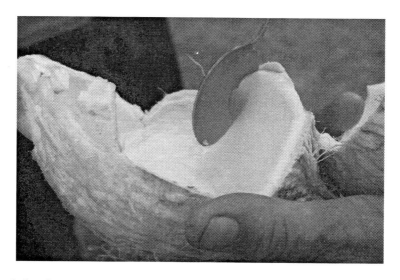

Pour the månha juice into a cup. Spoon the meat into the same cup. Add a little sugar to the meat and juice, and set it in the fridge. This is the perfect food after a day at the beach!

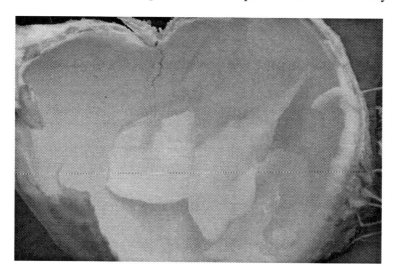

CRACKING A MATURE COCONUT

Using the BACK of a machete or cleaver, tap the center of the coconut at its circumference. Rotate the nut after every hit until the coconut cracks in half.

Save the coconut juice to drink later.

GRATING A COCONUT WITH A KÅMYO

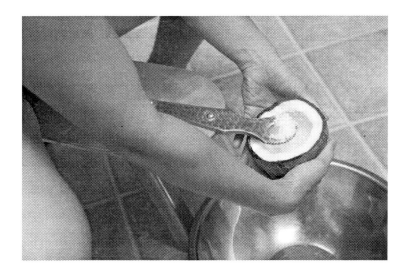

You would have to watch someone grate a coconut to see how it is done. The first shavings of coconut are the best because it is the sweetest and most moist part of the coconut! Grate till you get very close to the shell. Set aside the freshly grated coconut.

Don't throw away the shell! You can place them in the oven to dry out and remove all of the white flesh. Then, you can buff the outside / inside and smooth the edges. You now have the makings of a bowl or cup, and even the beginnings of a coconut bra! Also, the shells are used in traditional island dances for musical effects. The shells make for good bbq wood too.

Setting the Chamorro fiesta table

Below is a line-up of how a typical Chamorro fiesta table is set. This was a suggestion from my friend, Fe Thornton. It is a great idea as it is something we should be skilled in eh!

Front of table: *PAPER PRODUCTS*
                           STARCHES: *Rice*
                                        Titiyas
                                        Bread
                                        Plantain / Suni / Taro

- *PAPER PRODUCTS*
- *STARCHES:* *Rice*, *Titiyas*, *Bread*, *Plantain / Suni / Taro*
- *MEATS:* *BBQ meats*, *Fried meats*, *Ham*, *Roast beef*
- *FINA'DENNE'*
- *OTHER:* *Potato salad*, *Pancit*, *Shrimp patties*, *Lumpia*, *Empanåda*
- *FISH:* *Eskabechi*, *Fried / bbq fish*
- *KELAGUENS*
- *PICKLED:* *Cucumber / daigo*, *Kimchee*
- *SALADS*

Side tables:
- *SIDES:* *Soups*, *Sushi*
- *CARVINGS:* *Pig*, *Beef*
- *DESSERTS*
- *DRINKS*

122

Recipes

Read the entire recipe and watch the video before attempting to make the dish.

*Complete video demonstrations are available via a password-protected page at www.paulaq.com. Please e-mail Paula at rememberguam@paulaq.com for the password. In the **SUBJECT** line type: **PASSWORD** and the **ISB**N number from the back of the book. If you would like to purchase a DVD of the videos, please email Paula your request at rememberguam@paulaq.com.*

BOÑELOS

(bo-nye-lus)

Boñelos is of a mainly Spanish origin. Boñelos is also spelled buñelos, bimuelos, birmuelos, bermuelos, burmuelos, bunyols. A few countries, namely Nicaragua and Cuba, use yucca (tapioca) in their boñelos. Many countries including Mexico use yeast dough flavored with anise. Worldwide names for boñelos include filhos, andagi, fritole, lokma, oliebollen, loukoumade, and awwamaat.

Of course, the U.S. version of boñelos is the doughnut. For mainlanders, there are chocolate covered doughnuts, doughnuts with sprinkles on them, crème filled doughnuts, powdered sugar covered doughnuts, etc.

On Guam, some boñelos dough is similar to very thick cake batter, dropped into the hot oil from one hand. Other boñelos dough are rolled out, shaped, and fried in the oil. The Chamorro doughnuts include yeast doughnuts (rolled out dough, shaped into a circle or a twist, fried and covered with cinnamon & sugar), boñelos aga, boñelos dågo, boñelos kalamasa, boñelos lemai, and boñelos manglo / airee / pakyu.

Boñelos aga – This is the most popular boñelos for the Chamorros. Depending on the recipe, boñelos aga may come out a bit oily and flat, though delicious! Other boñelos aga will come out less oily and more round, still just as delicious! I prefer these banana doughnuts over banana nut bread! This batter is dropped from one hand into the oil.

Boñelos dågo and Christmas – a perfect combination. One of my fondest memories of having boñelos dågo (white or red yam) was when FBLG was an elementary school. The teachers would organize quad parties. One of the desserts we had was boñelos dågo – and there was even a Christmas song to go with it. This boñelos is not sweet. Hence, it is served with pancake syrup, anibat tuba (sweet tuba syrup), or "sugar water" (sugar dissolved in water).

Boñelos kalamasa – Use fresh, pureed pumpkin whenever possible. This is most tasty with the addition of pumpkin pie spice, cinnamon and vanilla. Boñelos kalamasa is also dropped from one hand into the oil.

Boñelos lemai – Apparently, this is a little more difficult to perfect. I first had these at a relative's bbq on Macheche hill. I would love to learn how to make this. I am not even sure if I could find breadfruit out here in North Carolina. This dough is rolled out, shaped, and then fried.

Boñelos månglo / airee / pakyu – This is actually the sweet flour titiyas dough, rolled out, cut into diamonds, and fried.

Boñelos yeast – Mmm, now this doughnut is the sugary – cinammony, sweet confection that kids sold door to door! Because this is a stiff dough, it is rolled out into a rope, shaped, allowed to rise, then deep fried.

BOÑELOS AGA

OMG – take me home!! A few months ago, I was sick to my stomach! Wouldn't you know one bag of boñelos aga made me feel much better!

INGREDIENTS

Set 1
1 ½ c. very ripe, smashed bananas (2-3 medium to large bananas)
½ c. sugar
1 t. vanilla

Set 2
1 ¼ c. flour (+1/8 c. more may be necessary)
1 t. baking powder

Set 3
Vegetable oil for deep frying

Tools: *large pot,   ladle w/ holes,   medium bowl,   colander,   napkins*

DIRECTIONS

1. Fill the large pot half way with oil. Heat the oil on medium heat.
2. Combine the smashed bananas, sugar, and vanilla.
3. Add 1 ¼ cup flour and baking powder. Mix thoroughly.
4. Depending on the ripeness of the bananas (water content), you may not need the remaining 1/8 cup of flour.
5. Check the thickness of the "cake mix like" batter. The batter should be a bit thicker than cake mix, but not at all like bread dough. Take a scoop in your hand. Drop it into the rest of the mixture. The scoop should retain some of its shape without completely

blending into the mix. It will slightly flatten out, but you should be able to see the outline.

6. If you are not sure, leave out the extra flour for now.
7. **Test your "batter dropping" technique.** Scoop a small amount of batter into the palm of your dominant hand. Make a circle with your thumb and fingers. Turn your "circled fingers" to drop some batter back into the bowl. This takes a little bit of practice. If you can squeeze the batter out and let the trail of batter fall onto itself in the oil, your doughnuts have a good chance of turning out round. If not, and the boñelos has a tail, the more crunchy parts to eat! You can always use two small spoons.
8. Drop about a teaspoon of batter into the oil. First, is the oil hot enough? If not, wait till it is hot enough, or turn up the heat.
9. The batter should turn into a puffy ball. The batter may fall to the bottom of the pot, but rise as it cooks. It will only stay at the bottom a few seconds. If it sits longer, the oil is not hot enough.
10. Test a large portion of batter. Scoop enough batter in your hand to form 1 doughnut. Drop it into the oil. The oil should be hot enough to cook the center of the boñelos and brown the outside of the doughnut, about 15 minutes.
11. Let cool. Open the doughnut and check to see if it is cooked. Check carefully as there will be chunks of banana in the boñelos. If in doubt whether there is enough flour, I would go ahead and add the remaining 1/8 cup of flour.
12. Fry the remaining batter and cool in a colander or napkin lined dish.
13. This will yield a small batch of boñelos, which should be quite soft even after it has completely cooled. If you don't think it is soft, leave out the remaining 1/8 cup of flour next time.

Making boñelos requires small adjustments to the dough depending on how much water is in the fruit, in this case bananas. This recipe is quite reliable. Do not add more flour than I have listed, unless you like your boñelos on the harder / firmer side. This recipe does not yield a very oily doughnut. There is a recipe out there for boñelos that gives an oily, but sooo yummy doughnut!

BOÑELOS DÅGO

(daw-goo)

I love the texture of this doughnut. While the dågo on Guam is a bit different (red dågo) from what one can purchase out here (white yam), it is close enough. Stateside, you can buy white dågo at Asian stores under a few names:

Japanese mountain yam – nagaimo, yamaimo

Chinese yam – huai shan, shan yao, or huai shan yao

Korean yam – ma

Dågo does have oxalate crystals on its skin. The crystals create an itchy sensation for humans. Research indicates a brief submersion in a vinegar-water solution should help to neutralize the crystals. If you decide to try this, don't keep it in the vinegar-water for too long or you may taste the vinegar in the finished product.

Traditionally on Guam, I have not heard of this practice. So, you can wear gloves or brave it out when skinning the dågo with a potato peeler. Otherwise, handling the batter with your hands does not seem to be a problem.

Dågo has a lot of water in it. Hence, all you need to make the batter is sugar and flour. Below is a picture of a Japanese mountain yam, a.k.a. nagaimo.

INGREDIENTS

Set 1
4.5 c. grated dågo (about 4 average sized yams)

Set 2
½ c. sugar
3 ½ c. all-purpose flour
¼ c. cake flour

Set 3
Oil for deep frying
Maple syrup, pancake syrup, sugar water, or anibat tuba for dipping

Tools: *large pot, ladle or tongs, cheese grater, colander, napkins, container for finished doughnuts*

DIRECTIONS

1. Pour oil into pot and heat on medium heat.
2. Skin the yams. Discard skins.
3. Grate yams.
4. Add sugar.
5. Add flour a little at a time to make the batter thick enough to drop from your hand.
6. Batter should pull away from the bowl but still be soft and sticky.
7. Drop a test doughnut into the oil (see boñelos aga for batter dropping technique).
8. Immediately after frying, the finished doughnut may not look cooked on the inside, but it is the dågo you are seeing.
9. Doughnut should be golden brown on the outside.
10. If doughnut does not rise to the top, use a fork to dislodge from the bottom of the pot.
11. **If doughnuts stick together, immediately separate them.**
12. **If they have browned quite a bit, do not separate the doughnuts. If you do, you will create an opening in the doughnut for the dågo to come out with a BAM!!! The water content will literally create a burst of moisture, which popping into the oil, will cause there to be quite an explosion of oil......as if you splashed water into the pot.**
13. Dip finished doughnuts in your choice of syrup.

After the boñelos dågo cooled off completely, I put some in the freezer in a Ziploc freezer bag. OMG, I thawed the boñelos then heated them in the microwave so they were nice and hot. Wow, with real maple syrup they were soooooo delicious! I loved them even more than when they were freshly made!

BOÑELOS KALAMASA

(ka-la-ma-sa)

It took me several attempts to figure this one out! But, after some advice from Auntie Daling and a few adjustments on my part, I've come up with this recipe – I LOVE IT! I love the delicateness cake flour gives to this boñelos!

INGREDIENTS

Set 1
1-15 oz. can pumpkin (or 1 2/3 c. fresh pumpkin)
1-12 oz. can evaporated milk (about 1 2/3 c.)
1 c. sugar
2 t. pumpkin pie spice
1 t. cinnamon
2 t. vanilla

Set 2
2 c. all-purpose flour
¾ c. cake flour
3 t. baking powder

Set 3
Oil for frying

Tools: *two medium bowls, whisk, large pot, colander, slotted spoon, small plate, napkins, baking pan*

DIRECTIONS

1. Fill pot half way with oil. Heat oil on medium heat.
2. Mix all of set 1 in medium bowl: pumpkin, milk, sugar, spices.

3. Combine the flours and baking powder in the other medium bowl. Add the dry mixture into the wet mix and stir to combine.
4. Refer to boñelos aga for "batter dropping technique."
5. Using one hand, test a mound of batter in the oil. Oil must be hot enough to cook the inside of the doughnut in about 12-15 minutes without burning the outside.
6. Once oil is hot, drop more batter into the oil. You must constantly turn the boñelos in the oil to cook / color the boñelos evenly. It should cook to more of a brown than a golden color.
7. Remove cooked boñelos to the colander then to a napkin lined baking pan.
8. This makes about 40-50 pieces depending on how large your boñelos are.

I used cake flour to lighten the batter. It gives the boñelos a very soft center. You can use just all-purpose flour. It may, however, be a bit dense in the middle.

BOÑELOS YEAST

Can you say "gof munngi?" This is definitely soooooooooo yum-yum! One of my mother-in-law's productions, this is a very soft, melt in your mouth doughnut!

INGREDIENTS

Set 1
3 – ¼ oz. pkgs. yeast
2 T. sugar
1 c. warm water at 110 degrees

Set 2
9 c. flour

Set 3
2 sticks unsalted butter, melted
1 c. warm, evaporated milk
¾ c. warm, whole milk
¼ c. olive oil

Set 4
2 eggs, beaten
1 c. sugar

Set 5
Oil for deep frying
1 ½ c. sugar for dusting
3 T. cinnamon for dusting

Tools: *large bowl,   2 medium bowls,   whisk,   large pot,   slotted ladle or tongs*

DIRECTIONS

1. Beginning with set 1, pour 1 cup water into large bowl. Add the 2 tablespoons of sugar and dissolve.
2. Sprinkle yeast over the water and let sit for a few minutes. Whisk to dissolve yeast. Set aside in oven for 15 minutes (DO NOT put the oven on).
3. In a separate bowl, beat together the 2 eggs and 1 cup sugar from set 4.
4. Add the 2 sticks melted butter, 1 cup warm, evaporated milk, ¾ cup warm, whole milk and ¼ cup oil to the eggs, little by little, whisking as you go.
5. Pour the new mixture into the yeast and completely combine.
6. Add half of the flour into the batter and mix with your hands. Add the remaining flour to form a slightly, sticky dough.
7. Allow this dough to rise, about 45-60 minutes.
8. Knead the dough a few turns (Do not over-knead as it will make the doughnuts tough). Allow the dough to rise another 45-60 minutes.
9. Fill pot 2/3 with oil and heat on medium to medium-high.
10. Divide the dough into equal portions.
11. Roll each portion out to form a long, thin log with a diameter measuring just over 1 cm.
12. Bring the two ends of the log together to slightly overlap, with the ends winding 2 times around. **PINCH** the ends to secure.
13. Roll all pieces out, giving the first batch enough time to rise, about 15 minutes.
14. Fry till golden on the outside.
15. Dough will float once in oil.
16. When done, remove from the oil. Sprinkle cinnamon and sugar over hot doughnuts.
17. Cool on a wire rack.
18. Store in an open container or in an opened paper bag.

CHALAKILES

(cha-la-kee-lis)

This is a yum-yum soup! It is quite a favorite at rosaries and nobenas. Chalakiles is a ground-rice and chicken soup, flavored with achote, garlic, and onions. I first made this soup during one of my college breaks....it turned out perfect!

INGREDIENTS

Set 1
2 c. UNCOOKED Calrose or short grain rice

Set 2
1 ½ c. diced onions
8 cloves garlic, minced
1 T. vegetable oil
½ c. chopped, uncooked bacon

Set 3
6 uncooked, chicken drumsticks
1 ½ t. salt
½ t. blackpepper
16 c. water

Set 4
2 T. achote seeds *(or 1 packet achote powder dissolved in*
1 T. vegetable oil)
2-3 t. seasoning salt
2 packets Goya
donne' or hot pepper flakes to taste

Tools: *large pot, strainer, cookie sheet with raised edges, blender, small plastic bowl*

DIRECTIONS

Preheat oven to 350 degrees.

1. Spread 2 cups rice on cookie sheet with a lip (raised edges).
2. Toast rice kernels till they are a golden / dark brown. Stir occasionally.
3. Once rice is golden-brown, remove rice from oven and pour into plastic bowl to cool.
4. Heat 1 tablespoon of oil in large pot.
5. Sautee onions and garlic in oil.
6. Add uncooked bacon if desired. Sautee for a few minutes.
7. Add chicken to the pot and allow to brown on one side for 3 minutes.
8. Sprinkle 1 ½ teaspoon salt and ½ teaspoon black pepper over chicken and stir.
9. Allow to brown on the other side for 3 minutes.
10. Adjust heat as necessary or stir chicken so as not to burn it.
11. Once chicken is browned, pour 4 cups water over chicken.
12. Cover the pot and bring to a boil. Let cook for 30 minutes stirring occasionally.
13. While chicken is cooking, pour 1 cup of the toasted rice into a blender. Pulse (there is a pulse button on the blender) only to "chop" rice kernels. DO NOT GRIND TO A POWDER!
14. Pour the ground rice into a small bowl.
15. Repeat with the second cup of rice.
16. Once chicken is cooked, pour another 4 cups water over boiling chicken.
17. Remove 1 drumstick at a time from the pot.
18. Remove / discard skin and bone.
19. Shred chicken with two forks. Return shredded chicken back to the pot of boiling water.
20. Repeat steps 17-19 with remaining chicken.
21. When all of the chicken is shredded, add the remaining 8 cups of water.
22. Pour all of the ground rice into the pot of boiling water.
23. The water will thicken as the rice cooks.
24. After about 10 minutes of boiling, suspend the strainer over the pot, about 1 inch into the boiling soup. Place the achote seeds in the strainer and stir to release the color / flavor. *(If using achote powder, mix the powder and 1 tablespoon of oil in a cup. Pour this paste into the soup.)*

25. Add the remaining seasonings from set 4.
26. Continue to boil the soup till the rice is cooked. Adjust seasonings to taste.
27. At this point, you can add more water if you want your soup runny. *(If you will be using this for empanada filling, do not add more water. Sixteen cups thus far is sufficient.)*
28. The chalakiles will thicken quite a bit in the fridge.
29. Leftover soup, if thick enough the next day, may be used as the filling for empanada.

CHAMORRO CAKE

I love this cake! Never mind the frosting! If you enjoy a nice balance of flavor-density-tenderness-aromatics and down-to-earth Chamorro goodness....without the "bells and whistles," this is the cake for you! Not to be mistaken for the **brohas** *(sponge cake), Chamorro cake is sometimes made with raisins. This cake is "an almost pound cake."*

I initially made Chamorro cake with regular flour and beat the eggs on medium speed of an electric beater. I really loved the result: a dense and heavy cake, very similar to pound cake. However, for the second attempt, I used cake flour and beat the eggs on high speed. My family preferred the second version. I would suggest you try the second version first, which is the recipe below. If you want something a little different, go ahead and replace the cake flour with all-purpose flour and beat the eggs on medium speed. The heavier, dense cake would be excellent for latiya!

INGREDIENTS

Set 1
Crisco to grease the cake pan
1/3 c. flour to dust the cake pan

Set 2
3.5 c. cake flour
1 ¼ t. baking powder

Sct 3
2 c. butter, MELTED
2 ¾ c. sugar
6 large eggs

<u>Set 4</u>
2 t. lemon extract
1 t. vanilla extract
1 ¼ c. evaporated milk

<u>Set 5</u>
2/3 c. raisins, optional

Tools: *small pot, large bowl, medium bowl, 9x13 cake pan, electric beater, napkin, a 2 cup measuring pitcher or larger*

DIRECTIONS

Preheat the oven to 350 degrees.

1. Using a napkin, grease the 9x13 pan with Crisco then dust with flour. Tap out excess flour.
2. In a medium bowl, combine the 3.5 cups flour and baking powder. Set aside.
3. Pour melted butter into the large bowl. Add the sugar to the butter
4. Beat the sugar / butter for 2-3 minutes till well combined.
5. Crack all the eggs into the measuring pitcher trying not to break the yolks. This step is really to simplify the addition of the eggs.
6. From the pitcher, pour 1 egg into the creamed sugar and beat on **HIGH for 1 minute** (a single egg will easily pour out).
7. Continue step #6 until all eggs have been completely incorporated. The resulting batter will be lighter in color and quite fluffy.
8. Add the lemon and vanilla extracts.
9. Beat on low to completely incorporate the lemon and vanilla.
10. Add 1/3 of the flour and 1/3 of the evaporated milk. Beat on LOW to partially combine.
11. Repeat #10 twice more with the remaining flour and milk continuing to beat on **LOW just till slightly combined**.
12. Using a spatula, finish mixing the batter by hand to prevent over-beating.
13. Pour batter into prepared cake pan and bake for 55-65 minutes depending on the oven.

14. Insert a skewer or butter knife in the center to test for doneness. Cake is ready when tester comes out clean.
15. Cool on a wire rack.

I am indeed a cake girl! The best cakes are those you can eat without frosting. I must say, in my years as a dessert enthusiast, this is the yummiest cake I have had! Some cakes are too rich, others require a frosting, many are too sweet, and a few are dry. The Chamorro cake, for me anyways, is perfect: perfectly flavored, perfectly sweet, perfectly textured. It is PERFECT as a meal itself!

CHICKEN ALA KING

I remember when you could find chicken ala king at many parties on Guam! Since I have been here in the states, I have not found this on the tables of many Chamorro gatherings. The original filling recipe that I started with was from a resident of Santa Rita. I didn't get her exact recipe. However, her technique is probably what is most valuable. Below is my tested recipe for the pastry and the filling. IT IS FABULOUS!

The pastry cups for chicken ala king must be mixed / fried before the filling is made. Hence, get all the ingredients measured out for the filling. Once the pastry cups are made, you can quickly get started on the filling. Remember, the filling and pastry cups are set side-by-side on the table or filled just prior to serving. Do not fill the pastry cups ahead of time or you will have a huge, soggy mess!

The pastry cups are made using rosette irons (sometimes called timbale irons / cups). Rosette irons come in various sizes and shapes. Some irons are actually cups that can hold sweet or savory fillings. Google "rosette irons" to find many on-line stores selling these tools.

PASTRY SHELL

The finished pastry cups for this specific recipe will last at least five days in a Ziploc bag. It was still very crunchy by the time I ate the last cup.

INGREDIENTS for pastry shell

Set 1
1¼ c. flour
½ c. cornstarch
1 t. salt
3 T. sugar

<u>Set 2</u>
¾ c. evaporated milk
¼ c. Budweiser beer
¼ c. water
2 large eggs

<u>Set 3</u>
Oil for deep frying

Tools: *iron cups, blender or food processor, fork, large pot, kitchen tongs, napkins, oil / sugar thermometer*

DIRECTIONS for pastry shell

1. Pour all liquids and eggs into the blender.
2. Add the dry ingredients.
3. Cover blender and pulse (press the "blend" button on and off).
4. Use a small spoon to scrape the edges of the blender, cover, and pulse again till smooth and creamy.
5. REFRIGERATE **overnight (two nights is fine).**
6. Heat the oil in a large pot to between **370 and 375 degrees.**
7. Line a large plate with napkins. Use this plate as the "tapping out oil" plate before dipping irons into the batter.
8. Dip the iron cups into the hot oil for about 2 minutes.
9. Tip cups over in pot to drain excess oil then lightly tap the cups on a napkin-lined plate.
10. Dip the iron cups into the batter AT AN ANGLE then level the iron out (otherwise, the bottom of the iron will not get completely covered in batter…..and the resulting pastry will have a hole)!
11. DO NOT go over the edge of the cups or the pastry will not fall off of the iron when cooked.
12. Count for about 75 seconds (depending on your stove). Lift the iron. The pastry should fall off.

13. If necessary, remove shell from iron with fork and continue to fry till browned on the inside (bottom) of shell.
14. LEAVE THE IRONS IN THE OIL in preparation for the next shell(s).
15. Remove pastry cups from oil with ladle or tong.
16. Cool on wire rack, bottom (solid) sides up.
17. The pastry will be a golden / dark brown so as to cook the bottoms of the shell.
18. There will also be some bubbling of the batter on the outside - bottom.
19. Makes about 25 pastry cups.

FILLING

INGREDIENTS for filling

<u>Set 1</u>
2 T. butter
½ c. finely diced onions
4 cloves garlic, minced
½ c. chopped celery

<u>Set 2</u>
32 oz. chicken broth, heated in microwave
1 medium Russet potato, diced (uncooked), soaked in cold water
1 c. frozen carrots / peas mix, thawed
1 c. canned corn, drained
1.5 c. cooked, chopped, chicken
½ c. green onions, chopped

<u>Set 3</u>
¾ c. left-over pastry batter

<u>Set 4</u>
¾ c. evaporated milk
2 T. butter
¾ t. black pepper
1 t. salt
1 t. seasoning salt

<u>Set 5</u>
3 boiled eggs, chopped

Tools: *large pot, large spoon*

DIRECTIONS for filling

1. Heat large pot. Add butter and sautee onions and celery. Add the cooked chicken.
2. Add the hot broth to the pot and bring to a boil.
3. Add potatoes and vegetables. Bring to a boil till potatoes are tender.
4. Add the green onions.
5. Lower the heat to a gentle simmer. Add the ¾ cup left-over pastry batter. Cook for two minutes.
6. When this is bubbly, add the evaporated milk and the remaining butter. Cook another two minutes.
7. Add black pepper and salt, adjust to taste.
8. Turn off the heat and add the chopped eggs.
9. Keep warm till ready to serve.
10. When ready to eat, pour filling into pastry cups and enjoy!!

This is a very thick and yummy filling!!

COCONUT CANDY

As I am "kåmyoing" (grating) the coconut to make coconut candy, I remember back to when my dad would be grating coconut. My siblings and I would ask for the initial shreds of the coconut because it was the sweetest and the moistest. This is the part of the coconut meat that is in direct contact with the coconut juice, the liquid inside the nut.

In 1999, while I was in Germany, I made coconut candy for the liberation celebration. I passed it around in spoons. I made the candy from memory, using only sugar and coconut. Though I caramelized the sugar, it was not sticky. Hence, I could not form it into coconut candy balls. I vowed to someday get this down pat.

Fast forward 2008, Holly Springs, NC. While I was experimenting and caramelizing the sugar / butter, I chuckle as I remember the coconut candy fiasco at Yigo Elementary School (early 1980's). Someone brought in salt instead of sugar. What a big surprise we had!

There are many variations of coconut candy. I was interested to see how other countries made theirs:

Malaysia – They slightly dry their coconut then mix it with sugar and evaporated milk. At some point, they color the coconut candy with food coloring.

Bahamas – Here, the recipe and directions are similar to some of the Chamorro coconut candy recipes. This is a boiled water method using vanilla, cinnamon, and baking powder.

China – The Chinese use brown sugar instead of white sugar. They wrap their coconut / sugar mixture in wonton wrapper.

Mexico – Their version of the candy boils shredded coconut, coconut milk, milk and sugar in a pot. Egg yolks and sherry are also added, followed by almonds as a garnish.

Philippines – Molasses is used. The candy is cooked when a little of the mixture hardens upon being dropped into cold water. This candy is individually wrapped in cellophane.

In summary, I did not come across as simple a recipe for coconut candy as how we make it on Guam....at least how I remember making coconut candy.

So, my friends, here is a tried and true recipe for coconut candy. This is the caramelized (dark) version.

INGREDIENTS

Set 1
2 c. sugar
1 T. butter
4 ½ c. grated, fresh coconut *(2 coconuts make about 4-5 cups. I would buy 3 if in the states, preferably at an Asian store. Most of the time, at least one coconut has spoiled).*

Tools: *cleaver or machete, kamyo, newspaper, cup, 2 large plastic bowls, large frying pan (non-stick would work best), long wooden spoon, tin foil, non-stick pan spray*

DIRECTIONS

PREPARING THE COCONUT

1. If you are lucky to be on Guam, you need to husk the coconut. Most stateside coconuts are already husked and you are left with the brown nut.
2. Take the back of the cleaver or machete and rap (tap hard) the coconut as you turn it in your hand. You want to split the coconut into two short halves. The coconuts I have seen in mainland stores have a partial "rap" line already marked. Catch the coconut juice with a cup and save it if you like the taste....drink up later.
3. If you don't have a kåmyo, find a good friend to buy you a blade on Guam. Then, find a nicer friend to make a bench for you....mine is out of stainless steel!

4. Lay the newspaper underneath the front portion of the kåmyo. It simply makes for an easy clean-up.
5. Place the large bowl underneath the blade of the kamyo. Rotate the coconut with both hands grating out the white "meat." BE CAREFUL! The kåmyo blade is SHARP!

MAKING THE CANDY

1. Heat the frying pan (a non-stick works great for easy clean-up and easy stirring) on medium.
2. Pour sugar into the pan and allow it to gradually melt. Stir constantly.
3. Add the butter when the sugar is partially melted.
4. Lower the heat. You need to melt all the chunks of sugar without burning it.
5. Carefully break the chunks of sugar apart by softly pressing on it with the thick edge of a wooden spoon.
6. Once all pieces of sugar have dissolved, increase the heat a little bit.
7. When the sugar is a really dark brown, add the coconut and stir.
8. The candy should be sticky. There should be more coconut than sugar.
9. Remove from the heat.
10. Pour the candy into a non-heat conducting, durable plastic bowl.
11. As the candy cools, it will thicken. Place in fridge for a few minutes to speed up the cooling process.
12. Spray a sheet of tin foil with pan spray.
13. Once coconut candy is slightly warm, form into one inch balls.
14. Let cool completely.
15. Enjoy this treat.......though sparingly because it is quite sweet!

What a way to travel back in time! My Auntie Lulu used to always make this at Grandma Cruz's house. Between this candy and boñelos aga, I will always REMEMBER GUAM!

EGGPLANT IN COCONUT MILK

This is a tasty way to prepare eggplant, courtesy of my dad and my brother Jun. Most people tend to bbq their eggplant. The bbq method yields very little eggplant to eat. My dad suggested I boil the eggplant instead. So, the recipe below is using eggplant that has been boiled. I found very long, (a foot and a half) thin eggplants at an Asian store. I boiled them in a large pot. The skin wrinkled up. I used the fork-tender test to check for doneness.

INGREDIENTS

Set 1
1.5 c. cooked eggplant, drained *(about 4 medium-large eggplants, boiled)*

Set 2
½ c. thick coconut milk
¼ t. lemon powder
¼ t. salt
½ c. finely diced onions
½ clove garlic, grated

Set 3
2 T. freshly squeezed lemon juice
donni' or hot pepper

Tools: *large pot, strainer, large bowl, small bowl, fork*

DIRECTIONS

1. Cook eggplants using your choice of cooking method till eggplants are fork-tender.
2. Remove / discard the outer skin and stems of eggplants with your fingers. Depending on how tender the eggplant is, you may use a fork to rake the meat, or the meat may just peel away in shreds.
3. Place all the peeled eggplant into a bowl. Allow eggplant to cool, draining excess liquids.
4. Add onions, salt, lemon powder, and lemon juice. Stir.
5. Add coconut milk and hot pepper.
6. Place in fridge till cold.
7. Before serving, do a taste test. Adjust accordingly.

EMPANÅDA

(im-pa-naw-da)

This is a great meal in itself, if you don't mind that it is deep fried. The filling is thickened chalakiles soup. The crust is achote colored masa-harina mix. There were days on Guam when little kids would go door to door selling empanådas and other goodies.

To Chamorros, this term conjures up a distinct, edible experience. When Chamorros yearn for empanåda, they imagine that orange-red, fried masa-harina crust enveloping a thick, shredded, chicken-speckled rice or cream of wheat, blasted by sautéed onions, garlic, and hot pepper mixture. Hard core dieters are putty within reach of these most sought after treats.....especially off-island!

I searched the internet to see how other countries make their empanåda. I was very surprised! Again, for Chamorros, an empanåda is an empanåda, a very unique food item. For many parts of the world, however, the word empanåda is generic. Some places use flour, masa-harina, or a combination of both for the crust. Some are fried, while others are baked. The fillings are a spectrum of the sweet and the savory.

Costa Rican Empanåda – This is the only country I found that used the empanåda press the Chamorros are familiar with. These Costa Rican empanadas, though using masa-harina for the crust, did not color their crust.

Veracruz Empanåda – This Mexican version uses masa for the crust, but it is rolled out. Minilla is used as the filling (a mixture of shark, olives, and spices).

Ilocos Empanåda – This is the only empanåda I found that used the achote (aka acheute) coloring in the crust. This is a Filipino empanåda where the crust includes rice flour. The filling is made of longganisa, veggies, and has an egg cracked into it. This empanada is immediately fried.

FILLING

1. Make the chalakiles soup on page 135.
2. Place to cool overnight in the fridge.
3. This soup will thicken even further in the fridge to the consistency necessary as a filling for empanada.

CRUST
(makes about 40 pieces)

INGREDIENTS *for crust*

Set 1
4 c. masa harina
1 packet achote powder
2 packets Goya seasoning *(found in the Hispanic section of the store, the one that says "Goya con y cilantro")*
3 t. seasoning salt

Set 2
4 c. water

Set 3
Oil for deep frying

Tools: *empanada press (or two flat-bottomed plates and rolling pin), wax paper, large Ziploc bags, several cookie sheets*

DIRECTIONS *for assembly*

1. Cut the wax paper into squares slightly overlapping the edges of the empanada press, about 45 pieces.
2. Place the masa harina, Goya, achote powder, and seasoning salt in a large bowl. Mix to combine.
3. Add the 4 cups of water to the mix.
4. Knead the dough to form a soft, non-sticky dough. Form dough into small balls, about the size of a golf ball.
5. Place a sheet of wax paper on the empanada press. Place a ball of dough on top of that piece, followed by the second sheet of wax paper.
6. Using the press, flatten the dough.
7. The thickness of the dough should be about 1/8 of an inch.
8. The dough should not extend beyond the empanada press.
9. Remove the top sheet of wax paper and save to use on the next empanada.
10. Put 2-3 T. of filling in the center of the dough.
11. If you like to eat a lot of fried empanada dough, put only two tablespoons of filling. If you like more filling instead of dough, then use a large amount of filling....careful to leave enough space to seal the empanada.
12. Fold the dough in half keeping / using the sheet of wax paper. Do not remove this piece of paper till you fry the empanada.
13. Seal the edges by bringing the edges of the empanada together and pressing with your fingers along the wax paper.
14. Freeze in a single layer (with the wax paper still on the empanada) on a cookie sheet. Once empanadas are hardened, you can store them in large Ziploc bags (still with wax paper on it).

COOKING THE FROZEN EMPANADAS

Tools: *large pot for deep frying,   colander,   tongs or frying ladle,   napkin lined tray*

1. Heat oil in large pot on medium heat.
2. When oil is ready, remove the wax paper from the **FROZEN** empanada.
3. Deep fry the empanada **WHILE THEY ARE STILL FROZEN**!! Do NOT thaw the empanadas or you will have quite a mess.
4. **DO NOT TOUCH OR MOVE** the empanadas till after 10 minutes of frying!!!! The crust needs to harden before you "move" the empanadas around…..if it doesn't harden first, you will have a big mess as well.
5. As the empanada cooks, it should tilt on its side.
6. Fry till golden orange, about 12-15 minutes.

KÅDDON MÅNNOK   (CHICKEN SOUP)

(kaw-dun   maw-nuk)

Mmmmm, this is cause for a rice throw-down with fina'denne' as the beverage!

INGREDIENTS

Set 1
1 T. vegetable oil
1 c. onions, roughly cubed
4 cloves garlic, minced

Set 2
4 lbs. chicken (I used drumsticks.)
***IF POSSIBLE, SOAK THE CHICKEN OVER NIGHT IN WATER WITH 3 TABLESPOONS
SALT. This will help to draw some of the blood out of the chicken.*
***Drain the chicken in a colander before using.*

Set 3
¼ t. salt
¼ t. black pepper
1 T. soy sauce

Set 4
48 oz. chicken broth (6 cups)

Set 5
1 potato, skinned, cubed (soaked in cold water)
2 cups roughly chopped cabbage (larger than onions)

Tools: *large pot,   large / long spoon,   colander*

DIRECTIONS

1. Heat oil in a large pot on medium heat.
2. Salt and pepper the chicken. Set aside.
3. Add half of the onions and half of the garlic to the hot oil. Sautee for a few minutes.
4. Add chicken to the pot. Turn heat up and let brown 2-3 minutes. Watch to ensure the bottom of the pot does not burn.
5. Stir and let brown again 2-3 minutes. Repeat one more time.
6. Add 1 T. soy sauce, stir and let brown for 2-3 minutes.
7. Stir and let brown again for 2-3 minutes.
8. Add remaining onions and garlic, stir.
9. Add chicken broth and stir.
10. Cover the pot to bring kåddo to a fast boil.
11. Remove cover and lower heat to a gentle simmer for 20 minutes.
12. Add the potatoes and boil till potatoes are fork tender.
13. Add cabbage and cook 2 more minutes.
14. Taste kåddo and adjust salt / pepper.

KÅDDON PIKA

(kaw-dun pee-ka)

Mmmm, a rich version of estufao! This dish is enhanced with coconut milk, fresh or canned. I remember eating this often. Some make it really hot, others make it palatable. You need a ton of rice!!! It is sooooo good with a whole, chopped up chicken: lots of bones to suck on and meat to eat....if I could only get myself to make a mess chopping the pecker up☺! Otherwise, I use drummetes / wings or drumsticks.

I like to soak my chicken overnight in water and salt to draw out the blood. This is not necessary, simply a personal preference.

INGREDIENTS

Set 1
2 lbs. chicken (8 drumsticks)
enough water to cover the chicken
3 T. salt

Set 2
1 medium onion, sliced
6 cloves of garlic, minced
¾ c. soy sauce
¾ c. vinegar
½ c. water
¼ t. black pepper

Set 3
1 T. vegetable oil
1 c. coconut milk
1 t. pepper flakes (local donne' if you have some)

Tools: *large bowl or Ziploc, large pot*

DIRECTIONS

1. In large bowl or Ziploc bag, soak chicken in salt and water overnight (optional).
2. Drain water.
3. Combine all ingredients from set 2 in the bowl or bag. Marinate chicken for 30-60 minutes.
4. Heat 1 tablespoon of oil in large pot.
5. Sautee chicken and some of the onions / garlic for 20 minutes till browned. Add a little of the marinade to the sautéing chicken as needed.
6. After 20 minutes, pour the remaining marinade into the pot.
7. Cover the pot and gently simmer for another 20 minutes.
8. Add half of the hot pepper.
9. Uncover the chicken and continue to simmer for 20 minutes allowing the water to evaporate to reduce the liquid. Skim fat from the surface.
10. Add coconut milk and pepper flakes to the chicken.
11. Let simmer for 3 minutes then turn heat off.
12. Adjust pepper to taste.

<u>KELAGUEN</u>

(ke-la-gwin)

Kelaguen - a noun and a verb. In Chamorro, to kelaguen something is to "cook or finish cooking" in lemon juice / lemon powder (if no lemon powder, use unsweetened lemon Kool-aid), finely diced yellow onions, chopped green onions, hot pepper, salt, and a little bit of water (when necessary). We commonly kelaguen chicken (kelaguen månnok – finely chopped chicken), shrimp (kelaguen uhang – crushed shrimp), deer (kelaguen binådo – thinly sliced), beef (kelaguen kåtne – thinly sliced), imitation crab (shredded), and yes, even Spam (crushed - Treat works great too). For most kelaguens, we add freshly grated coconut.

Kelaguen is similar to ceviche (cebiche or seviche from Latin America). Ceviche dishes, however, use some type of large-chunked seafood (clam, mahi-mahi, shrimp, octopus, tuna, squid, marlin, and mackerel). Depending on the country, ceviche may also include avocado, coriander, parsley, cilantro, and tomatoes.

Kelaguen sounds quite like kilawin, the Filipino version of ceviche. Many of the kilawin recipes I reviewed used fish or pork snout. Also, kilawin typically is made with vinegar, calamansi juice, garlic and ginger.

SHRIMP KELAGUEN

I ate shrimp kelaguen once, a very long time ago. For the most part, I would bypass shrimp kelaguen simply because there were always so many other choices at a Chamorro party. Chicken kelaguen, crab kelaguen, and kelaguen binådo were my primary selections for this yummy lemon dish.

I called my dad because he and my mom always made shrimp kelaguen while I was growing up. He advised to de-vein and de-tåki the shrimp (remove the shrimp poop). Rinse it good. Most importantly, he stated, "When you make shrimp kelaguen, SMASH THE SHRIMP with the bottom of a heavy cup." I heeded his teachings and OMG, my shrimp kelaguen, mind you this was the first time I EVER made it, was the bomb! Even my brother, Jun (Paul), thought it was "very good kelaguen"....he commented several times about how good it was. Well, praise about my food, from my brother, a better cook than myself........ I did well!

Below is my recipe, courtesy the teachings of my dad.

INGREDIENTS

Set 1
3 ¼ c. smashed shrimp *(2 lbs. frozen, uncooked, headless shrimp, with shell on)*

Set 2
1 t. salt
2.5 t. lemon powder
½ c. finely diced, yellow onions
1 c. freshly grated coconut
¾ c. fresh lemon juice (3-4 medium to large lemons)
hot pepper to taste

Tools: *flat-bottomed, heavy cup or bowl,   colander,   medium bowl,   small plate*

DIRECTIONS

1. Pour shrimp into colander and rinse under cool water.
2. Peel off shells and clean tåki *(poop)* on the outer curve of shrimp. Rinse as you do this.
3. De-vein shrimp on the inner *(concave)* curve and remove the tail *(where the "dåggan" of the shrimp is....there is a clump of tåki in there).* Rinse as you do this.
4. Once all the shrimp is de-veined and de-tåkied, give a final rinse under cool water. *(Some people pour boiling water over the shrimp. DON'T DO THIS. It will cook the shrimp a bit, and the shrimp will not smash as it should).*
5. Place 1-4 pieces of raw shrimp on a small plate. Smash with the bottom of a heavy cup or bowl.
6. Put all the smashed shrimp in a medium bowl.
7. Add the salt, lemon powder, and lemon juice.
8. Mix thoroughly till shrimp has changed from grey to light pink. This may take a few minutes as the lemon begins to cook the shrimp.
9. Add onions, hot pepper, and coconut.
10. Mix thoroughly.
11. Taste shrimp. You should taste the lemon more than the salt.
12. Add more lemon juice if necessary, more salt, and hot pepper if desired.
13. Kelaguen should be lemony, not salty. You should be able to taste the richness of the coconut as well.

SPAM KELAGUEN

We don't find Spam kelaguen on party tables very often. You will most likely find this as a dish made for the home. If you really want some kelaguen, you love Spam, and you are too lazy to chop chicken, this is a quick, tasty recipe.

INGREDIENTS

Set 1
1 – 12 oz. can reduced sodium Spam
2-2.5 t. lemon powder
¼ c. minced onions
2 T. green onions
¼ - ½ t. hot pepper

Tools: *medium plastic bowl, wooden spoon*

DIRECTIONS

1. Place Spam in the bowl and crush with one hand.
2. Add onions, lemon powder, and hot pepper.
3. Mix all ingredients with a wooden spoon, adding more lemon powder and hot pepper to taste.

PANTOSTA

Pantosta, or toasted bread, for the Chamorros, is bread meant to be dipped in coffee! Growing up, we bought pantosta instead of making it ourselves. Or, my Grandma Cruz would toast sandwich bread, and that worked as a substitute.

Here is a delectable recipe from Mom Q. Making pantosta is a time consuming endeavor. The following recipe yields a very large batch of dough. It takes a long time to roll each piece, bake the entire batch, and an even longer time to dry / do the final baking.

One thing you may try is to use your favorite bread recipe. Perhaps you can try a ready-made, refrigerated dough....following the baking / browning / hardening procedures below.

The resulting pantosta, using this recipe, takes a little longer to soak up the coffee...but it is sooo delicious. Also, this is extra yummy when you dip this pantosta in Country Crock Spread......OMG!

Hm, butter and pantosta...reminds me of the sweet Navy biscuits with a lot of butter on top...YUM!

INGREDIENTS

Set 1
1 large vanilla pudding box *(the cooking kind)*
1¾ c. milk + 3 c. *(required for the pudding recipe on box)*

Set 2
3 – ¼ oz. pkgs. Active Dry yeast
1 c. warm water at 110 degrees
1 T. sugar

<u>Set 3</u>
2 eggs, room temperature
1 ½ c. sugar
Dash of salt

<u>Set 4</u>
12 ½ c. all-purpose flour

Tools: *3 medium bowls,   2 very large bowls,   several cookie sheets,   non-stick baking parchment, non-stick pan spray*

DIRECTIONS

1. In a medium bowl, make the box of vanilla pudding according to directions on the box, adding the extra 1¾ cup of milk. **Set in the fridge overnight.**
2. From set 2, pour the warm water and sugar into a medium bowl, stirring to dissolve the sugar. Sprinkle the 3 packages of yeast over the water. Stir to dissolve. Set aside in the oven (DO NOT turn oven on).
3. In a separate medium bowl, combine the eggs, sugar, and salt from set 3.
4. Remove the pudding from the fridge and add to the egg mixture.
5. Pour this egg / pudding combo into the dissolved yeast.
6. Stir to combine. Transfer this mixture to the very large bowl.
7. Slowly add the flour to the wet mix till incorporated. Initially, add only the 12 cups of the flour, four cups at a time, to form a slightly, sticky dough. If the dough feels really wet, go ahead and add the last half cup of flour. DO NOT add more!
8. Spray the second very large bowl with pan spray.
9. Place the dough into this bowl. Set the bowl in the oven for 60 minutes (DO NOT turn oven on).
10. Punch the dough down and let rise again for another hour.
11. Spray several cookie sheets with pan spray or use baking parchment
12. Use a ¼ cup measuring cup *(preferably with a thin rim)* to scoop dough portions out. Divide each ¼ cup portion in half. Or, you may simply pull pieces of dough out estimating the size.

13. Roll each piece into very thin, long, ropes about 1 cm thick and 6 inches long.
14. Place on cookie sheet about 2 inches apart. Let rise on counter-top as you roll out more dough.
15. Heat oven to 300 degrees.
16. Bake a sheet of dough till each piece of "bread" is BARELY browned, about 17 to 20 minutes.
17. Remove "bread" from cookie sheet and cool completely on a wire rack.
18. Repeat #16 and #17 till all pieces of dough have been partially baked.
19. **Reduce the oven heat to 200 degrees. Allow a few minutes for the temperature to drop.**
20. Carefully fit as many pieces of "bread" directly on both oven racks. REMEMBER, THE OVEN IS HOT! You can let the pieces touch each other.
21. The "bread" will have to dry / bake for about 5 to 6 hours. During this time, it will darken, cook, harden, and shrink. Check pantosta every 1.5 hours. How dark is it? How hard is it?
22. Once "bread" has taken on a much darker color, press a few pieces between your fingers. If it is not very hard, continue to cook in oven.
23. Pantosta is done when it is COMPLETELY hardened.
24. This drying process may take 4-6 or more hours depending on how thick your dough is, how hot your oven is, and humidity.
25. Cool on a wire rack and store in Ziploc bags.
26. Makes about 110 pieces if you use the ¼ cup method above.

You may also bake some of dough for soft, sweet bread. Once you have pre-baked the number of pantosta you want, turn the oven up to 350 degrees. Bake the bread till nicely browned, about 14 minutes (I simply shaped all of my dough into pantosta logs, but baked the last 3 sheets of dough for soft bread). While the soft bread is baking, the pre-baked dough is cooling off. This recipe yields delicious soft, sweet bread, especially the next day, warm out of the microwave! Remember to decrease the oven temperature down to 200 degrees when you are ready to dry the pantosta.

POTO

(po-too)

These steamed rice cakes are made in many countries!

Malaysia – Putu Piring: ground rice flour is patted into a mold, followed by palm sugar then covered with more rice flour.

China – Kuih Tutu: similar to Malaysia, but uses a variety of sweetened fillings including coconut and peanuts. This is also called white sugar sponge cake

Phillippines – Puto: closer to what we make on Guam, except they may use Bisquick, egg whites, ube, and coconut milk. They may line their puto molds with banana leaves. The Filipinos also like to color their puto with food coloring.

Of course, the Chamorros put their own twist on it by using tuba instead of water. In my experience, it has been quite a challenge to make poto without tuba. Traditionally, the Chamorro poto is made with ground rice, tuba, and sugar. It ferments / rises overnight from the compounds in the tuba. For now, this is as close to poto as I have been able to get without using tuba.

I have tried to make poto so many times! In college, the mush didn't even rise out of the mini-cupcake pans (I did not have the individual poto molds).

While visiting my good friend Nancy White in Colorado Springs, Colorado, she ordered puto from her Filipina friend. Mmmmm, though it was a different kind of Filipino puto, it was soooo good. Unfortunately, we could not get the recipe. It was not like the Filipino recipe which included Bisquick.

So, this is not quite the final recipe, but it is a great one for now. You will need to set aside a few hours time to dry, grind, and sift the rice / rice flour. After all of that, it takes just a few minutes to mix and 30 minutes to rise or proof. I love the texture of this poto....it is chewy like

Chamorro poto. This poto is also white like ours. The only thing I have to work on now is the "fermented" taste.

INGREDIENTS

<u>Set 1</u>
5 c. Calrose / short grain rice
enough water to cover rice

<u>Set 2</u>
1 ¾ c. coconut milk
¼ c. water
1 T. coconut vinegar
1 T. + ½ t. baking powder
pinch of salt
¾ c. sugar
Crisco for greasing muffin pans

Tools: *several medium bowls, colander, steamer basket, non-stick mini muffin pans (holds 12), fine strainer, 2-3 cookie sheets with raised edges, kitchen towel to cover steamer, good coffee grinder (about $20.00), paper napkins*

DIRECTIONS......*grinding the rice to make homemade rice flour.*

1. Soak rice overnight in medium bowl with just enough water to cover the rice.
2. Drain rice in colander for two hours.
3. Spread rice on cookie sheet in about ¼ inch to 1 centimeter thickness.
4. Turn oven to warm or very low heat, the lowest heat setting on your oven.
5. Place rice covered cookie sheet in oven just for 5 minutes.
6. Remove from oven and let dry. The warm sheet will help to dry the rice.
7. Pour ½ cup of dried rice into coffee grinder. Grind on "fine" setting.
8. Pour ground rice into medium bowl.

9. When you have about 4 cups of ground rice, place through the fine sieve….this is the first round of sifting.
10. You will be left with coarse grains of rice. Set aside the coarse pebbles in another bowl.
11. Once you have sifted the ground rice-flour the first time, SIFT IT AGAIN FOR THE SECOND TIME.
12. Measure out **3 cups of twice sifted rice-flour.** If you do not have enough, regrind the coarse bits *(from #10)* and sift that twice as well.

DIRECTIONS……*making the poto*

1. Pour the 3 cups of homemade rice flour into a medium bowl
2. Add the rest of the ingredients and stir well to mix thoroughly. Let sit for 30 minutes. It will not be bubbly.
3. The mixture will seem kind of runny….it's ok! It will work.
4. Cover and heat the water in the steamer to a rolling/fast boil and keep it at that heat.
5. Grease the mini muffin pans / tart molds with a napkin and Crisco.
6. Stir the poto mixture.
7. Fill each mini muffin space ¾ full.
8. **BE CAREFUL OF STEAM WHEN YOU REMOVE THE COVER. Set the muffin pan in the steamer basket!**
9. Place the kitchen towel over the basket *(will prevent water from dripping onto poto)*. Set the cover atop the towel.
10. Steam for 20 minutes.
11. If using aluminum / steel molds, you may need a cold water bath. Use a cake pan or cookie pan with raised edges. Fill with ice water and set aside.
12. BE CAREFUL OF STEAM.
13. Remove the cover then remove the towel. BE CAREFUL OF STEAM.
14. Remove the muffin pan / tart molds *(use cold water bath if not using non-stick molds)* and let cool.
15. Fill the other muffin pan and repeat above steps.
16. Poto from first pan should remove quite easily.
17. ENJOY!!!!!!

POTO II

The following poto is not as close to the Chamorro poto as the previous recipe. However, it is so delicious and easy, I had to include it.

INGREDIENTS

Set 1
2 c. Bob's Red Mill White Rice Flour *(available at most supermarkets)*
¾ c. sugar
1 T. baking powder
pinch of salt

Set 2
2 c. coconut milk
1 T. coconut or palm vinegar

Tools: *medium mixing bowl, steamer basket, mini muffin pans (holds 12) or individual poto molds, kitchen towel to cover steamer, silicone gloves made for hot pans / pots, wire rack*

DIRECTIONS

1. Prepare steamer basket: fill with water and bring to a fast, rolling boil.
2. In a medium bowl, combine the flour, sugar, baking powder, and salt.
3. Add the milk, water, and vinegar. Mix completely to form a smooth batter.
4. Using a napkin, grease pans / molds with Crisco.
5. Fill each mold ¾ full.
6. Keep one steamer basket on the countertop *(off of the boiling water)*.
7. Place pan / mold into the basket. Then, place the basket over the pot of boiling water. Cover with kitchen towel. Put the steamer cover over the towel.
8. Steam for 18-20 minutes.

9. Simultaneously remove the basket, towel, and cover from the boiling water. Be careful of the steam when uncovering and removing the cover / towel.
10. Take the pan / mold out of the basket and place on wire rack.
11. Remove individual poto using a small spoon. Set pastries on wire rack to cool completely.

POTO III

This is the recipe used on the video.

This is the closest poto recipe I have come across that is DELICIOUS, EASY TO MAKE, and REPLICATABLE. It is a combination Mom Q. came up with.

INGREDIENTS

Set 1
1 ¾ c. Bob's Red Mill White Rice Flour *(available at most supermarkets)*
½ c. all-purpose flour
½ c. LOW-FAT Bisquick (or Bisquick Lite)
¾ c. sugar
1 – ¼ oz. pkg. Highly Active Yeast
2 c. warm water (110 degrees).

Tools: medium mixing bowl, steamer basket, mini muffin pans (holds 12) or individual poto molds, kitchen towel to cover steamer, silicone gloves made for hot pans / pots, wire rack

DIRECTIONS

1. In a medium bowl, combine all the ingredients listed in set 1.
2. Let sit for 1 hour.
3. Prepare steamer basket: fill with water and bring to a fast, rolling boil.
4. Using a napkin, grease pans / molds with Crisco.
5. Fill each mold ¾ full.
6. Keep one steamer basket on the countertop (off of the boiling water).
7. Place pan / mold into the basket. Then, place the basket over the pot of boiling water. Cover with kitchen towel. Put the steamer cover over the towel.

8. Steam for 15 minutes.
9. Simultaneously remove the basket, towel, and cover from the boiling water. Be careful of the steam when uncovering and removing the cover / towel.
10. Take the pan / mold out of the basket and place on wire rack.
11. Remove individual poto using a small spoon. Set pastries on wire rack to cool completely.

ROSETTES

Growing up on Guam in the 80's, I could always find these cookies at parties. It was exciting to see them because they were so pretty! Many, many years ago I bought my rosette irons from Lujan's store in Anigua. They are one of my prized possessions! If you cannot get them on Guam, they are available from online stores / catalogs. Do a Google search for "rosette irons" and you should find them. I am not sure how and when the irons came to be on Guam. Was it through our early European discoverers or did the rosette find its way via the USA?

Rosette making dates back to the Iron Age. Some countries dust their rosettes with regular sugar or powdered sugar, others add cinnamon to the sugar while a few countries flavor the batter with vanilla or almond extracts.

*In Salamanca, Spain, there is such a cookie called a **floreta**. The floreta is formed from heavy irons called "de forja." The picture of the floreta looks as if it has a thicker "shell." The iron appears to have greater height (or depth if you will), hence, a taller cookie.*

*The Danish call rosettes a **struvor**.*

Making the rosettes is time consuming. This recipe yields about 28 rosettes. If you use the double rosette iron, you should make two batches of this recipe. The container you will pour the batter into has to be large enough to fit the double iron. One batch of the batter will not be deep enough to submerge the irons. If using a large food processor, you can simply double everything and make it at one time. If you use a blender, make 2 batches of the batter (DO NOT DOUBLE IT IN THE BLENDER. You DO NOT have to wash the blender in-between). On the other hand, you can simply attach just one of the rosettes to the handle and use a smaller container, thereby only needing to make 1 batch of the batter.

***This batter needs to sit in the fridge overnight** so plan accordingly. I left my batter in the fridge for 2 days and it was fine!*

INGREDIENTS

<u>Set 1</u>
4 T. butter, melted

<u>Set 2</u>
1 c. flour
2.5 T. sugar
¼ t. salt
¾ c. whole milk
1 egg
1.5 t. vanilla

<u>Set 3</u>
Vegetable oil for deep frying
2 c. sugar for dusting
¼ c. cinnamon for dusting

Tools: *blender, frying thermometer, rosette irons, large / deep pot, napkins for draining oil, wire cooling racks, wax paper, container for dusting, tong, fork, container wide and deep enough for the irons*

DIRECTIONS *for making the batter*

1. Combine all the ingredients from sets 1 and 2 in the blender.
2. Cover blender and pulse to thoroughly mix the batter.
3. Pour the batter into a container.
4. Lift the container slightly off of counter-top. Allow the container to drop down on the counter. This helps bring air bubbles to the surface to pop. You may also use a fork to prick / pop the surface of the batter.
5. Let batter **sit in the fridge overnight**.

COOK THE ROSETTES

1. Line the counter with wax paper slightly larger than your wire rack.
2. Line a large plate with napkins (to tap out excess oil from the irons).
3. Mix the cinnamon and sugar in a pan (a cake pan for example) and set aside.
4. Fill a pot about 2/3 full of vegetable oil and heat between **370 to 380 degrees**.
5. Heat the irons in hot oil for 2 minutes.
6. Remove the batter from the fridge.
7. Using a spoon, gently run the back of the spoon through the batter to "mix"….trying to avoid making bubbles. Discard the spoon.
8. Tap the irons on the napkins to drain excess oil.
9. Immediately dip AND HOLD the iron in the batter, careful not to go over the top of the rosette iron (otherwise you will not be able to remove the cookie as a whole).
10. Keep the iron in the batter for about 10-15 seconds to let the batter form onto the iron.
11. Remove iron from the batter and immediately place the battered-iron **deep** into the oil for about 60 seconds.
12. Because cook-top temperatures vary, you will have to find a happy medium of temperature and time.
13. Lift the iron out. The rosette should fall off the iron itself. If not, use a fork to push the rosette off the iron.
14. Once the rosette falls off or is removed from the iron, let the iron HANG OFF THE EDGE OF THE POT still immersed in the oil. This will keep the irons heated and ready to use. Once you get the hang of it, you may be able to cook two rosettes at the same time (using only one iron).
15. While in the oil, flip the rosette such that the design faces up (to avoid removing a cookie with oil caught in the shell).
16. Remove the cookie from the oil and place directly into the pan of cinnamon and sugar, face down. You will only sugar-coat the side with the design.
17. Place the rosette face up on the wire rack to cool.
18. Reheat the iron in the oil for 1 minute….if you forgot to keep the irons in the oil.
19. Repeat the above steps till the batter is used up.
20. Once all cookies are cooled, store in Ziploc bags for several days.
21. WARNING! These cookies can be addictive. Take one or two, and put the rest away!

SHRIMP / SPAM PATTIES

I have never been a shrimp patties kind of girl! It is sooo oily for me.....every shrimp patty I have ever tasted. However, they are delicious! Shrimp patties are not a regular item at a bbq like kelaguen or lumpia. I can tell you though, these babies go quickly! Many people seem to like them the next day too! A friend said that the best shrimp patties are the ones that you can eat straight out of the fridge...COLD! Well, my recipe was good hot and cold on the counter. I could not keep it in my house long enough to fridge overnight, translated: I absolutely had to give it all away so I would not eat it! Mm, but I sure liked it better cold than hot. I think it is one of those things where the flavors need time to mingle.

This would be the first time I'd make shrimp patties. So, I called my mom. She gave me her recipe, but it was for a large batch and no specific measurements of flour and baking powder. I did some research, took her advice, and made a composite shrimp patties recipe. Also, from my baking / pastry background, I decided to add an extra egg than what most recipes advised. Think about cream puff dough, the French crueler doughnut. These are recipes with lots of eggs. The center of a good shrimp patty reminds me of the above......it is more "eggy" than "floury".

Most patties are made with a bag of mixed veggies: carrots, peas, green beans, lima beans and corn. My mom suggests cutting the green beans into thirds. I don't like frozen green beans and lima beans. I simply replaced them with celery.

My mom says that the finished batter should be thick enough such that it holds together on the spoon. You should NEED to use another spoon to push the batter off into the oil. I was not exactly sure what she meant, so I erred on the side of caution: I did have to use another spoon to push the batter off, but, some pieces of vegetables would fall off at the edges of the spoon anyway.

Once you spoon the batter into the oil, the patty should rise to the top within a few seconds. If not, you may need to increase your heat. Also, STIR the batter before every new batch is put in the oil.

INGREDIENTS

Set 1
3 large eggs at room temperature
¾ c. evaporated milk

Set 2
2 c. frozen carrots and peas mix
1 c. canned, drained, sweet corn
½ c. celery, finely diced
½ c. onions, finely diced
3 cloves garlic, minced

Set 3
¾ c. diced Spam
1 c. cooked, chopped shrimp
1/3 c. mashed shrimp

Set 4
1 1/3 c. all-purpose flour
3 t. baking powder
1 t. salt
½ t. black pepper
¼ t. garlic powder

Tools: *large pot for deep fry, frying ladle, 2 adult dinner spoons, medium bowl, napkin lined plate, napkin lined dish, colander*

DIRECTIONS

Preheat oil to medium heat.

1. In a medium bowl, gently beat the 3 eggs using a wire whisk. Add the ¾ cup carnation milk and mix to combine.
2. Pour all the veggies / spam / shrimp into the bowl and mix.
3. Add the flour, baking powder and seasonings to same bowl and thoroughly combine.
4. Test 1 spoonful (adult dinner spoon) of batter in the hot oil.
5. Watch for how the patty rises and puffs up.
6. The patty should rise quickly and puff into an oblong shape.
7. Fry to a golden color and place in a colander or napkin lined dish. If making a large batch, some people put the patties in a paper bag.
8. **Remember to stir the batter** before putting another batch in the oil.
9. As you cook the batter, the patties may not cook / rise like the first batch. Add 1 T. of flour and just under ¼ teaspoon of baking powder to the remaining batter. You may also have to increase your heat on the stove-top.
10. Repeat #8 and #9 as necessary.

SUSHI – GUAM STYLE

Yum! Of course, the best sushi is from a Japanese sushi house……..easily found on Guam. However, when off-island one must make due. Sushi, Guam style, in addition to the veggies, includes sweetened eggs, daigo (yellow radish), imitation crab, spam, or hotdog.

INGREDIENTS

Makes 10 sushi logs

Set 1
4.5 c. uncooked, short grain (Calrose) rice

Set 2
½ c. + 2 T. rice vinegar
3.5 T. sugar

Set 3
8 eggs
3 T. sugar
3 T. water

Set 4
Approx. 6 inches of a long, **whole daigo** (yellow dyed radish)
        sliced length-wise into strips
2 **avocados**, peeled, sliced lengthwisc
2 long **carrots**, peeled, sliced lengthwise into strips
1 **cucumber**, peeled, sliced into strips lengthwise
choice of **"meat"**: spam, hotdog, cut into strips
choice of **seafood**: imitation crab, raw tuna, raw salmon, cooked shrimp

<u>Set 5</u>
10 seaweed sheets for sushi (sold in most grocery stores and Asian stores)

Tools: *sushi mat, plastic wrap, large bowl, non-stick pan (preferably a rectangular or square one), pan spray, rice cooker or large pot, 1 cup measuring utensil*

DIRECTIONS

1. Cook rice in a rice cooker or on the stove top. Leave in the pot and set aside. You will need the rice to be hot!
2. Cover the sushi mat with plastic wrap.
3. Prepare all vegetables / "meat" / seafood accordingly, see set 4. Set aside.
4. In a medium bowl, gently beat 8 eggs, 3 tablespoons sugar, and 3 tablespoons of water.
5. Spray non-stick pan w/ pan spray. Heat on low.
6. Pour lightly beaten eggs into pan and cook very slowly, so as not to brown the eggs.
7. When the top of the egg is set, flip over in the pan.
8. Allow eggs to cook completely.
9. Remove eggs from the pan as a whole.
10. When cool, cut into strips 1 centimeter wide.
11. Measure 8 cups of hot rice into a large bowl.
12. Pour the rice vinegar and sugar over the rice.
13. Using a rice scooper, fold rice onto itself so as to combine, somewhat smearing / smashing the rice.
14. If you don't have a rice scooper, use a baking / mixing spatula.
15. Continue this until the rice is barely warm.
16. Place a sheet of seaweed on the prepared sushi mat.
17. Spoon and spread a scant one cup of rice over the seaweed to a ¼ inch thickness.
18. About two inches up from the bottom of the roll, line your veggies / meats ensuring that each left / right end has a piece.
19. Take the bottom of the roll up and over the filling.
20. Using the mat, roll the sushi into a tight cylinder. Set aside.
21. Repeat #16 through #20 for remaining ingredients.

22. If consuming immediately, go ahead and slice each roll about a half inch thick. If eating later, wrap each roll in plastic wrap.
23. Sushi is best eaten the same day. Day old sushi is ok. Two days old sushi, well, edible, but you will notice the rice starting to harden slightly.

TITIYAS

(ti-tee-dzas)

When a Chamorro wants titiyas, it is the flour version, the corn version, the fading (Federico) version, or the exquisite, månha titiyas. These delicacies are often ¼ inch thick. The titiyas may be cut into diamonds or left as a large, round disc. Titiyas fadang, one I have never tried, is not as popular. In fact, you may rarely, if ever, find this titiyas as the seed from this plant (cycads palm) must be processed properly to avoid poisoning.

TITIYAS MAI'ES

(my-is)

Corn titiyas is typically eaten with kelaguen, though can be eaten with any kind of meat or "chessa" (food the bbqers eat up while bbqing).

INGREDIENTS

Set 1
4 c. masa harina mix
2 T. sugar
1 t. salt

Set 2
3 ¾ c. water

Tools: *large bowl,   large non-stick pan,   empanada press or rolling pin,   wax paper, cooling rack*

DIRECTIONS

1. In large bowl, combine masa, sugar, and salt.
2. Add water and mix well to form a soft dough.
3. Knead dough in the bowl for a few minutes.
4. Divide dough into equal pieces. Shape into the size of 2-3 golf balls.
5. **Preheat a non-stick pan to medium heat.**
6. Cut about 20 pieces of wax paper slightly larger than the empanada press.
7. Place one sheet on the bottom half of the press.
8. Put one ball of dough on the wax paper.
9. Lay a second sheet of paper on top of the ball.
10. Close the press and squeeze to flatten the dough about ¼ of an inch thick.
11. If you do not have an empanada press, you may also roll the dough between the two sheets of wax paper using a rolling pin.
12. Peel the top piece of paper away from the flattened dough. Prick dough gently with a fork.
13. Keeping the bottom wax paper intact, flip the titiyas dough side down into the pan.
14. Remove the wax paper.
15. **COUNT 30-45 SECONDS THEN FLIP TO THE OTHER SIDE.**
16. Don't cook the first side too long otherwise the titiyas will not **LOOK** the way it is supposed to look on the other side. Be careful not to break titiyas on this first flip.
17. Let brown on the second side then flip to the initial side to brown and finish cooking.
18. Cut titiyas into diamonds or squares.

Esta ki

In closing…..

Folks say it's the journey that counts, not the end result. I'll have to agree! My work on "Remember Guam" has taken longer than anticipated, but it has been quite rewarding.

I started on "Remember Guam" in the summer of 2006, a year before I opened my personal training studio, CIRC FITNESS. My time, my resources, and my energy have been divided, stretched, and pulled to a new threshold.

Finally, I have completed my book. I am so touched by all the stories and memories people have shared. I am truly the richest person alive as my dedication and determination to complete "Remember Guam" have given immortality to those who took the time to write.

Thank you for remembering my island. I am so grateful to have had the honor of putting together this collection. Dånkolo na Si Yu'us Ma'ase (thank-you very much) to all who have contributed their precious memories.

My next book, *Chamorrita Passions,* has also been in progress since 2006. It is simply a historical romance novel, a love story intended to bring to life Guam's history, culture, and traditions. It is quite vivid and explicit throughout. Read on, and enjoy a few pages of this book (less the romantic / seductive scenes), which is yet to be completed.

For more recipes, order my cookbook, A TASTE OF GUAM, via my website, www.paulaq.com. While there, check-out a few recipes on video. The second edition of A TASTE OF GUAM is brewing! Oh, what fun that will be: full color and more Chamorro eats!

Keep abreast of my next few books through my "crumb" on the web. Email me at pquinene@paulaq.com if you have any questions or comments.

Chamorrita Passions

A passion for each other, a passion for life....

Written by
Paula Ann Lujan Quinene

Author's note: the following novel is still in its very early stage. The excerpts below may change by the time the novel is published.

Chamorrita Passions

A passion for each other, a passion for life....

Her uncles had brought this soldier down to their cave. Blood covered his body from head to toe. She was the only one in there. Jesi's family was able to keep this place a secret since the Japanese invaded Guam over two years ago. The cave was well hidden in the thickness of the jungle, the ocean on one side. The trek down to the cave was masked by the draping vines. It had been a while since she sneaked away to the cave, yet everything was still the same. They brought rice, some clothing, blankets, medical supplies, and other necessities down before the Japanese started bombing, December 8, 1941....

"Jesi, Jesi," she was broken out of her trance. "Maila hao hagå-hu." It was Uncle Juan calling her over to the soldier. "Gotti este taiguini," he motioned her to hold the towel against a bleeding wound on the man's forearm. Uncle Juan examined the rest of the soldier's body for any serious cuts. He sure had a huge bruise on his forehead. It's probably why he's unconscious. Uncle Juan gave Jesi some bandages to wrap and secure the injury. "Nåna's training will surely be put to use now," Jesi exclaimed.

Her grandmother, Tan Chai, her mother's mom, was a suru-håna, or medicine woman. Nåna could heal most illnesses brought to her for treatment. Jesi was next in line to take over the family tradition, or so her mother wanted, like her mother, grandmother, and great grandmother before her. It's not that she did not want to learn the ways of her ancestors. Jesi, however, wanted to do more than just medicine.

Uncle Juan and Uncle Ton had cut away the soldier's clothing while Jesi sifted through the first aid supplies. Her uncles worked carefully to remove the metal piercing his body. They cleaned and covered his private areas then motioned for Jesi to come over. Jesi proceeded to clean the rest of his body, especially, all the open wounds. Though much of the bleeding had stopped, she took extra care to do a thorough cleaning job. Jesi knew his risk of infection was high, so she ensured to cleanse and bandage properly. As she gently wiped his face, he could barely open his eyes. "You are safe. It's alright." her voice was calming. His eyes circled the cave, barely coherent, "My uncles brought you down here. You were injured and bleeding. You'll be fine!" He tried to get up, but felt a throbbing pain in his head, "No! You're hurt!" Jesi said this with such firmness it surprised even her. She gently pressed her hand against his chest as he struggled to get up.

**

January 1945

During the military recovery efforts, Johan traveled quite a bit throughout the island. "Not sure what I'll do today," he muttered. He hopped into his military jeep and started on his way. The aftermath of the war on Guam was devastating. As he drove through the streets, he saw Japanese prisoners of war cleaning up debris. It was the oddest thing that one of them was posing with a smile for a military photographer, perhaps glad the war was over, and they were still alive. Johan saluted the soldiers on guard.

Down the ways, he saw the remnants of a church with a huge, gaping hole on the front wall. "It must have been a beautiful church," he whispered. He thought about the sun shining through the painted glass on the arched window. Johan drove about five miles when he came across three boys on a carrabao (kabåyu). They rode it as one would ride a horse. Two of the boys were shoeless. "Amazing," he thought. The boys must have been younger than nine or ten, riding what was really a horned bull. Johan reached into his pocket for gum. "Here boys," he reached out and gave them each a piece of Doublement gum. "Si Yu'us Ma'åse," each boy said, beaming with smiles and gratitude. Johan since learned that meant thank-you.

Before Johan knew it, he was pretty close to the Taimanglo's property. Johan couldn't help but be drawn to her. Jesi. She was always on his mind. She took great care of him during his treatment, though she remained distant. Her father and brothers kept him so busy away from their property. Johan was a good person, at least he thought so. He wasn't sure if it was because he was not of Chamorro descent or because he was ten years older. They never told him to stay away from her. Johan thought perhaps it was a mixture of reasons: gratitude for the liberation, anger that it took so long, resentment for the extreme military presence. Whatever it was, he made a point to give back to these people who nurtured him.

Johan had packed some flour, sugar, salt, and butter to bring to Tan Chai and the other women of the family. He absolutely loved what the Chamorros called titiyas. It was a thick, sweetened version of a tortilla, a hundred times more delicious! He also brought the men some tools, nails, and beef jerky. The Chamorros did not have very much of these basic items from the mainland. Their local produce and livestock had also perished or been destroyed. He hoped this would bring a bit more joy to them.

"Håfa Adai," pure delight to his ears, Johan recognized that voice anywhere. "Håfa Adai Jesi," he grinned. "Håfa tatat manu hao," he spoke in Chamorro. One of the Chamorro men helped him learn some words. He wanted to impress her, to show her that he cared enough to learn her language. "Here, I brought some ingredients for the family," he said. "Harina, asukat, asiga yan mantakiya," Jesi pointed excitedly to each of the items. "Harina, asukat, asiga yan mantakiya," he repeated back to her. "Gof maulek," she said. "Very good," Jesi translated. "Come on, they will be so happy to see you. The family will be so appreciative! They will make you some titiyas, it seems to be one of your favorites, no?" she said. "Yes, it is. It is very good with that chicken and onions mix, kelaguen?" Johan replied. "Kelaguen is made using chicken, shrimp, beef, or deer. Deer is my favorite. One day you will have to try it with deer," Jesi advised. "Now then, you will have to make it for me!" Johan exclaimed. She smiled one of her brilliant, beautiful smiles. His heart melted every time.

Johan showed respect to those who were elder to him. He brought their hand to his forehead or kissed them on the cheek. Tan Chai was happy to see him. "Hi boy," she said. "Ñora Tan Chai," he replied. "Johan brought us some goodies. He loves your titiyas, mom," Jesi said as Johan åmenned Mrs. Taimanglo. "Mås dångkolo na si Yu'us Ma'åse adai, Johan. Esta tåya nu este siha," Jesi's mom thanked him. Jesi's six year old cousin, Anke, was running around the living room. Johan gave him some Doublement gum. "Si Yu'us Ma'åse," the little boy said. Johan rustled his hair.

This man was after her daughter's heart she thought. Mrs. Debbie Taimanglo realized, at this moment, that the soldier was falling for her daughter. She was not too happy about this. Her daughter was only sixteen. She should be marrying a Chamorro boy. Her father would be less happy. Mrs. Taimanglo will seek answers with prayer. She wanted a good life for her daughter. Jesi seemed to be happy, to enjoy life on the island, she always has. But, Jesi is growing into a young woman who will one day have her own family. The world is changing. As much as she treasured the suruhåna ways of her mom, she realized that Jesi must do more and be more than she or Tan Chai has ever been. Soon, Jesi would have to make her own decisions.

Tan Chai quickly went to work at making titiyas. Jesi and Johan helped Mrs. Taimanglo plant some fruit and vegetable trees on the ranch: laguanå, åtis, etc.

"Håfa pon choggue pågo?" asked Tan Chai. Jesi looked at Johan and said, "Grandma is asking what are you going to do now?" "I wanted to see if you needed help with anything and perhaps drive around the island. I am on-pass today" Johan exclaimed. Jesi translated this for her mom and grandma. "Where are Chief and the boys?" he addressed the matriarchs. Jesi said that they were out picking some wood, tin, and coconut leaves to reinforce their home; perhaps build a new, smaller house. "Grandma lost her house, and she wants to rebuild it close to the beach," commented Jesi. "I saw some stacks of wood on my patrol yesterday. I could go get some," he said. Jesi jumped at the opportunity to go with Johan. After all, she was just out earlier with her brothers doing the same thing. "Kao siña hu tattiyi si Johan potfabot?" she requested, her eyes unable to mask her excitement. "Sigi" her mom replied inadvertently. "Lao koni si Anke ya un adahi hamyo." Jesi kissed and hugged her mom. It was too late for Mrs. T to change her mind. She could not keep Jesi at home forever. Besides, Anke was going with them.

This was going to be a fun outing. She didn't mind Anke tagging along. He was such a clown for a little six year old. "Are you sure this is ok? I mean, I don't recall your dad ever letting you go without your brothers," he asked Jesi. Before starting the jeep, he looked over at the door of her house. Her grandma was coming out with something. "Munga maleffa ni i titiyas," she said. Johan gathered it meant 'take your titiyas' or something close to it at least, as he kindly accepted the package. It was warm and smelled so good. "Sigi, sigi," she said, chasing them away. "Hu guaiya hao Nåna! Adios!" Jesi blew a kiss to her grandma as Johan turned the jeep to leave.

Most Chamorros were very strict with their daughters. Tan Chai remembers the night when she was whipped for secretly meeting Jesus, Jesi's grandpa, after nightly prayer. One day, she was pinched so hard when her father saw Jesus simply walk past her house. She was not of age to have a boyfriend yet, barely fifteen years old. Tan Chai vowed during those years never to treat her daughters like that. She did eventually marry her love, smiling as she remembered the life she had with Jesus.

Tan Chai brought Deborah up in a less punitive environment. She was strict, but more receptive to the emotional needs of a young girl. They both raised Jesi to be ......

Jesi insisted that they drive to southern Guam and then tour on foot, climbing a few small hills. There were paths cleared to take the carrabao out to eat. There were also paths to secluded swimming areas. Jesi desperately needed to swim. "Oh, first, let's climb to the top of Mt. Jumuyong Månglo. Do you remember that one?" she asked. "Sure do," Johan replied. "Do you have some water? We could have a picnic at the top," she beamed. His heart was putty with her every smile. He would do anything and everything for this Chamorro girl. "Anke, you up for a climb?" she asked her cousin. "Uh huh," he retorted, a little smirk on his face.

Johan reflected back prior to his assignment to Guam. He had studied a little about Guam: the victory over Spain and the military governors appointed by the U.S. Johan was not so enthused to leave the United States, but duty called. Most of his friends were in Hawaii or sent to Europe. Now, he knew it was meant to be. He's had some experience with girls and women in his years, but nothing serious. He was too busy with studies, the military, and helping his family. Johan knew, from the moment he opened his eyes in the cave and saw her, that this was his soul-mate. He couldn't explain it, he just knew. There was something in her eyes, something in her touch. Call it instinct if you will. Johan has learned that he should trust his instincts. Jesi seemed to like him as well, and he sensed some deeper feelings.

It took a little while to reach the top of the mountain. Lucky thing he brought his machete, a gift from a local friend. "Wow, I have never been to the top of a mountain. This is no small hill Jesi. Can you swim down there?" he asked, pointing towards the bay at one end of the island. "A climb down will get you there, a climb back up will get you out," she said smartly. She held Anke's hand as this was the boy's first hike up. There were some clouds in the sky, and it was a nice relief from the sun. "We need the rain," Jesi commented. "One day when Anke is not with us, we will have to cross that path over there," she said pointing to her left.

"Time for titiyas," Anke announced. They all sat down and enjoyed the titiyas grandma made. "And she gave us something else you'll like!" Jesi handed over the container of kelaguen.

References

Bank of Guam. "History of the Bank." <u>BANK OF GUAM the people's bank.</u> 2007. Bank of Guam. 10 March 2009. <https://www.bankofguam.com/about/history.aspx>.

Casamar International. "Casamar Guam Inc." <u>CASAMAR Oceans of Dependability.</u> 2008. Casamar International. 10 March 2009. < http://www.casamarintl.com/guam.html>.

Salvador, Xenie. "Queen of the past….and the present." Pacific Daily News, 21 July 1994.

Sanchez, Pedro C. <u>Guahan Guam The History of our Island.</u> Agana, Guam: Sanchez Publishing House, 1998.

UOG. "History of UOG." <u>UNIVERSITY OF GUAM.</u> 2007. University of Guam. 10 March 2009.

<u>Wikipedia: The Free Encyclopedia.</u> 22 December 2008. Wikimedia Foundation. 10 March 2009. http://en.wikipedia.org.

Index

Memoir Years

Other

Participant Names

Recipes

SPECIAL FEATURE

Special Feature

My newest sister-in-law, Viktoria Karamov Lujan, married to my brother Paul Edward Lujan, Jr. (a.k.a. Jun), is sharing her family's recipe for Apple Cake and Moscow Salad. Both are recipes Viktoria remembers from her childhood years. I couldn't help myself! These are two very delicious dishes that I had to share with my readers!

Viktoria is originally from Azerbaijan, a small country directly on the Caspian Sea, part of the former Soviet Union. She and her family, however, were forced to flee to Moscow, then Germany. It is refreshing to meet someone who is also away from her home, who has memories from a time and a land that her children may not be able to experience. Sharing her recipes is a tribute to our culture, our heritage, and our roles as wives, mothers, and daughters! It is indeed a blessing that we as women possess the skills, the knowledge, and the desire to preserve, protect, and share our heritage through food.

I must say, it is a wonderful opportunity to spend this time with Viktoria and learn about her life: the foods she grew up with, her parents and grandparents, her traditions, etc. It helps me appreciate more the value in preserving and sharing my heritage, that of the CHAMORROS!

APPLE CAKE

I really love this cake! Through all my years of eating dessert, this ranks in my top three. It is rustic, simple, not too sweet, not too rich, and quick to prepare. The danger, however, is that one (I) can really eat half of this cake all at once!

INGREDIENTS

Set 1
5 eggs
½ c. sugar
½ t. vanilla
¾ c. unsalted butter, softened

Set 2
1 ¼ c. all-purpose flour   *(plus ¼ cup flour for the cake pan)*
1 t. baking powder

Set 3
½ c. chopped walnuts   *(plus a few walnut halves to decorate the top of cake)*
3-4 apples
juice of half a lemon

Tools: *2 medium bowls,   electric beater,   Crisco,   8 inch round pan,   napkin,   cake plate*

DIRECTIONS

Preheat oven to 350 degrees.

1. Prepare apples. In a medium bowl, mix the juice from half a lemon with three cups ice-cold water. This will prevent the apples from turning brown.
2. Peel each apple. Slice into ½ inch thickness, discarding the core.
3. Place slices into the ice-cold water. Set aside.
4. Using a napkin, grease the cake pan with Crisco.
5. Sprinkle ¼ cup flour into pan. Turn pan to coat it entirely with flour. Shake out excess flour.
6. In the other bowl, beat together the 5 eggs, ½ cup sugar, and the ½ t. vanilla.
7. Add the ¾ cup butter to the egg mixture and beat till very well combined.
8. Add 1 ¾ cup flour, 1 teaspoon baking powder, and walnuts to the wet mixture.
9. Beat all together till well mixed.
10. Spread half of the prepared batter into the cake pan. Arrange apple slices over the batter (saving four slices to decorate the top).
11. Spread the rest of the batter over the apples.
12. Decorate the top of the cake with the remaining apple slices and walnut halves.
13. Bake for 30 to 40 minutes or till toothpick inserted in center comes out clean.
14. Allow cake to cool for 10 minutes.
15. Remove cake from pan.
16. Cake is ready to serve hot.

I love this cake cold!!

MOSCOW SALAD

This is such a refreshing salad! While I love the potato salad we make on Guam, this Moscow salad is a combination of wonderful bursts of flavor!

INGREDIENTS

Set 1
3 large, hard boiled eggs, peeled, diced
3 small, white potatoes, boiled, peeled, diced
3 long carrots, par-boiled, peeled, diced

Set 2
5 baby dill pickles, diced
1 regular sized cucumber, diced
½ a small onion, diced
1 large can green peas, drained

Set 3
2 T. chopped parsley
2 T. chopped cilantro

Set 4
¾ of a large apple, core discarded, diced *(use lemon juice & ice-water bath if dicing apples ahead of time to prevent browning)*

Set 5
3 T. mayonnaise
enough sour cream for a slightly creamy texture
salt & pepper to taste

Tools: *large bowl,   container with cover,   large pot,   colander*

DIRECTIONS

1. Boil then dice the ingredients as noted above.
2. Viktoria actually puts her potatoes, unpeeled carrots, and raw eggs into one pot to boil all at once.
3. Allow all boiled, diced ingredients to cool (place in fridge if necessary).
4. In a large bowl, combine all ingredients from sets 1 through 4. Lightly mix them together.
5. Add the mayonnaise. Add enough sour cream to make a slightly creamy mixture. Stir it all together.
6. If you prefer a more creamy salad, add more sour cream accordingly.
7. Add salt and pepper to taste.
8. Refrigerate overnight for best results.

Paula Ann Lujan Quinene

Ah, Remember Guam has been an absolute blast! I am fortunate to have been able to complete this project. The collection of memories, stories, letters, and interviews are priceless and I am grateful I can share them with you!

I hope you find the recipes and videos easy to follow. There are as many subtle differences for Chamorro food as there are the cooks who make them. The recipes that are my own are based on what I can remember them to be while I was growing up on Guam. The recipes contributed by family and friends are their own variations. All recipes have been tested by yours truly!

You may notice there is a common theme in my two books, *A Taste of Guam* and *Remember Guam:* FOOD! I love Guam food! Keeping with this theme, my third book, Chamorrita Passions, is my work of art that will include nuances of foods / recipes. This historical, romantic, and seductive novel will encompass Guam and the Chamorro culture pre, during, and post World War II. This novel will be available for purchase in a few years! Keep in touch via my website, www.paulaq.com.